Homelessness in the UK

Series Editor: Cara Acred

Volume 262

Independence Educational Publishers

First published by Independence Educational Publishers
The Studio, High Green
Great Shelford
Cambridge CB22 5EG
England

Copyright

Photocopy licence

British Library Cataloguing in Publication Data

Homelessness in the UK. -- (Issues ; 262)
1. Homelessness--Great Britain. 2. Homeless persons--
Services for--Great Britain.
I. Series II. Acred, Cara editor.
362.5'92'0941-dc23

ISBN-13: 9781861686770

Printed in Great Britain

MWL Print Group Ltd

Contents

Chapter 1: About homelessness

Chapter 2: Young and homeless

Chapter 3: Tackling homelessness

Introduction

Homelessness in the UK is Volume 262 in the ***ISSUES*** series. The aim of the series is to offer current, diverse information about important issues in our world, from a UK perspective.

ABOUT HOMELESSNESS IN THE UK

Many people who have experienced homelessness describe feeling as though they are 'invisible' when living on the streets. This book raises awareness of homelessness in the UK, exploring its causes and effects. It also examines the problems faced by those who are young and homeless, as well as considering different types of homelessness and how we might tackle the issue.

OUR SOURCES

Titles in the ***ISSUES*** series are designed to function as educational resource books, providing a balanced overview of a specific subject.

The information in our books is comprised of facts, articles and opinions from many different sources, including:

⇨ Newspaper reports and opinion pieces

⇨ Website factsheets

⇨ Magazine and journal articles

⇨ Statistics and surveys

⇨ Government reports

⇨ Literature from special interest groups

A NOTE ON CRITICAL EVALUATION

Because the information reprinted here is from a number of different sources, readers should bear in mind the origin of the text and whether the source is likely to have a particular bias when presenting information (or when conducting their research). It is hoped that, as you read about the many aspects of the issues explored in this book, you will critically evaluate the information presented.

It is important that you decide whether you are being presented with facts or opinions. Does the writer give a biased or unbiased report? If an opinion is being expressed, do you agree with the writer? Is there potential bias to the 'facts' or statistics behind an article?

ASSIGNMENTS

In the back of this book, you will find a selection of assignments designed to help you engage with the articles you have been reading and to explore your own opinions. Some tasks will take longer than others and there is a mixture of design, writing and research-based activities that you can complete alone or in a group.

FURTHER RESEARCH

At the end of each article we have listed its source and a website that you can visit if you would like to conduct your own research. Please remember to critically evaluate any sources that you consult and consider whether the information you are viewing is accurate and unbiased.

Useful weblinks

www.alabare.co.uk

www.bigissue.com

www.centrepoint.org.uk

www.crisis.org.uk

www.depauluk.org

www.eyh.org.uk

www.homeless.org.uk

www.homelessuk.org

www.mungosbroadway.org

www.nosecondnightout.org.uk

www.shelter.org.uk

www.streetlink.org.uk

www.thepavement.org.uk

www.qha.org.uk

About homelessness

What is homelessness?

What is homelessness?

Homelessness is about more than sleeping on the street. Homelessness means not having a home and includes rough sleepers, as well as people who are staying with friends or family temporarily or in overcrowded, unsafe or insecure accommodation. Other people who might be eligible for help as homeless people include those who are living in conditions that are harmful to their health or who are at risk of violence or abuse in their homes. You can find out more about what homelessness means by visiting the Shelter website (www.england.shelter.org.uk).

How many people are homeless in the UK?

It is very difficult to know exactly how many people are homeless in the UK. This is because many homeless people sleep in out-of-sight locations or in squats or on the sofas of friends or family members and do not receive any support from homeless services. Despite this, we know that the number of homeless people has risen significantly since 2009. There were an estimated 1,247 people sleeping rough in 2009 and 1,768 people sleeping rough in 2011[i]. 51,640 households were in temporary accommodation on 30 June 2012[ii]. The dramatic increase in homelessness is thought to be due to a combination of rising unemployment, home repossessions and the effects of cuts to housing benefits forcing people out of privately rented housing[iii].

Why do people become homeless?

People do not become homeless because of personal or moral failings. Some of the main causes of homeless include relationship breakdown and domestic violence, mental or physical health problems, and substance misuse. People who are leaving institutions are also more vulnerable to becoming homeless, including people leaving hospital, prison, the armed services or care. About a quarter of people who are homeless have been in local authority care, four in ten rough sleepers in London have spent time in prison and 3% of rough sleeping and single homeless people are British ex-service personnel[iv]. Other reasons why people become homeless include a history of unemployment and the high cost of accommodation. Crisis has some excellent information about the causes and consequences of homelessness here.

Single homelessness and hidden homelessness

The Hidden Truth about Homelessness report found that the majority of single and homeless people in the UK are hidden. Hidden homeless people were found to be staying in squats, sofa surfing or sleeping rough. Single homeless people were also found in backpacking hostels, in caravans or tents pitched unlawfully, in privately run homeless hostels and in prisons and hospitals about to be discharged and with nowhere to go. Of the single homeless people who sleep rough, many sleep in out-of-sight locations and with little support from homeless services. Many single homeless people experience multiple ways of being excluded from society including long-term unemployment, mental and physical health problems, poor literacy, experience of the care system, disrupted education and substance misuse problems.

Homelessness and mental health difficulties

Over 70% of people using homeless services report experiencing mental distress. A mental health crisis can make it very difficult for some people to look after their home and can impact on their ability to work full time. Sudden admission into hospital means that people with mental health difficulties often have very little time to prepare for their home to be looked after, and benefits can sometimes be reduced or stopped after four weeks in hospital. The highest rates of mental health difficulties are found among rough sleepers and young homeless people, and over two thirds of rough sleepers have both mental health and substance misuse problems[v]. You can find out more about housing and mental health by visiting the Mind website.

Women and homelessness

About one in ten rough sleepers are women and around 45% of households accepted by local authorities as having priority needs for housing, and 41% of households in temporary accommodation, are single women with dependent children. In a typical day around 3,615 women and 3,580 children are supported in a refuge-based service in England[vi]. Sadly, government cuts have led to an increase in women being turned away from women's refuge services due to a lack of space, leading to more women rough sleeping or hidden and homeless[vii].

Domestic violence is the single most quoted reason for women becoming homeless, although physical or mental health problems lead to many women being homeless too[i]. Women who have become homeless after fleeing an abusive relationship are especially vulnerable to experiencing further abuse[viii].

'The research shows how many homeless women have experienced domestic and sexual violence and are not only homeless because of that abuse, but are often re-victimised in their attempts to keep a roof over their heads – forced to trade sex for somewhere to sleep or the promise of safety.' Nicola Harwin, chief executive of Women's Aid

References

[i] Homeless Link: Rough Sleeping – Key Facts March 2011

[ii] Communities and local government: Statutory Homelessness: April to June Quarter 2012, England

[iii] *The Guardian*: Homelessness rise of 14% 'just tip of iceberg'

[iv] Crisis: About homelessness – Causes and consequences

[v] National Mental Health Development Unit: Factfile 2 – Mental health and housing

[vi] Homeless Link: Statistics On Homeless Women – A Summary Of Key Facts And Figures September 2010

[vii] *The Guardian*: Cuts force domestic violence refuges to turn victims away

[viii] Women's Aid: Crisis report on homelessness – Women's Aid view

⇨ The above information is reprinted with kind permission from Quaker Homeless Action. Please visit www.qha.org.uk for further information.

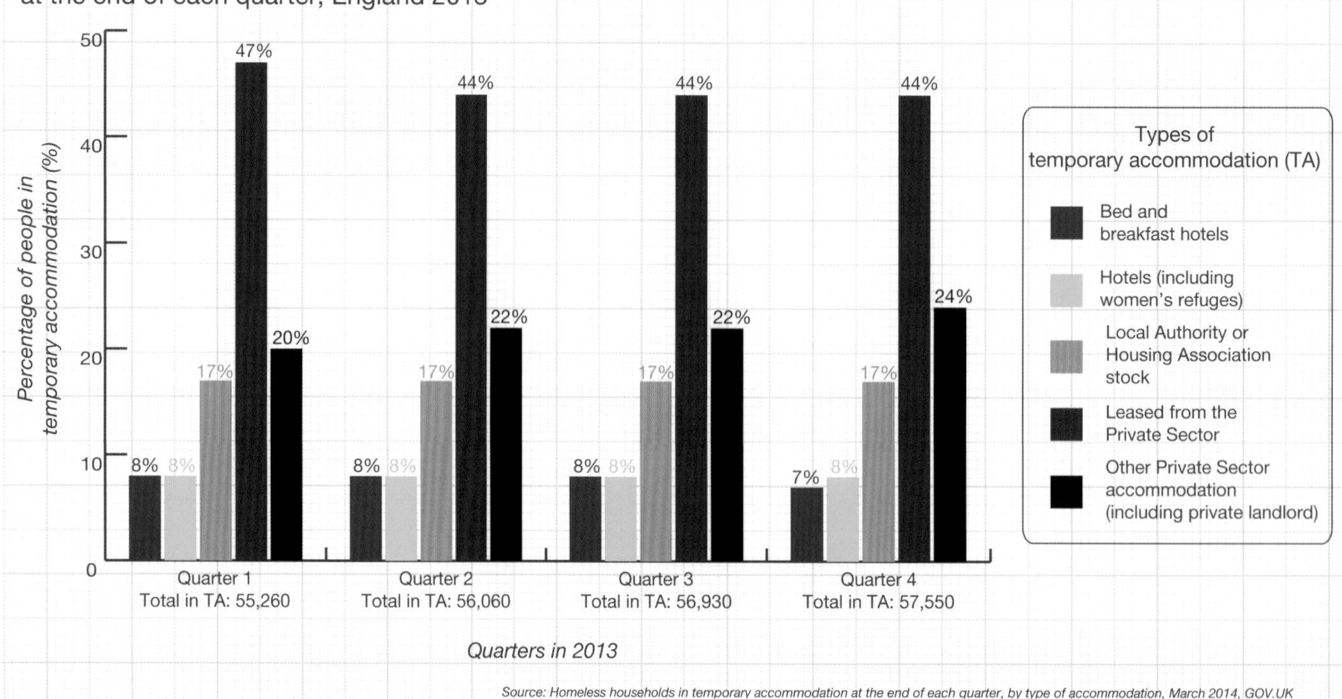

Statutory homelessness

If you become homeless, you might expect your local authority to provide you with accommodation, if only on a temporary basis. However, not all homeless people are entitled to housing, and this varies depending on which part of the UK you live in.

Even if you are entitled to housing, it may be some time before you are allocated permanent accommodation. In the mean time you will be housed in 'temporary accommodation'.

Who is entitled to housing?

In England, Scotland and Wales only 'statutory homeless' people are entitled to housing. This means you:

- are 'eligible for public funds' (this will depend on your immigration status)
- have some sort of connection to the area covered by the local authority, known as a 'local connection'
- can to prove that you are 'unintentionally homeless' (that it is not your fault that you became homeless)
- can prove you are in 'priority need' (the definition of which varies between the different nations and which will be abolished altogether in Scotland by the end of 2012).

Only once you have passed these stringent tests will you be considered statutorily homeless and only then do local authorities have a duty to house you. This is known as 'the main homelessness duty'.

'Priority need' definitions

If you are eligible for public funds, have a connection to the local area and can prove you are 'unintentionally homeless', you will then need to prove that you are in 'priority need' in order to be considered 'statutorily homeless'.

In the UK, 'priority need' was originally defined in the 1977 Housing (Homeless Persons) Act. This has since been refined and expanded in England and Wales, as well as Scotland, where it was abolished altogether at the end of 2012.

England

The 1996 Housing Act refined and expanded the definition of a household in 'priority need' in England (and Wales) so as to include:

- a pregnant woman
- dependent children
- someone vulnerable as a result of old age, mental illness or handicap or physical disability or other special reason
- someone homeless or threatened with homelessness as a result of an emergency such as flood, fire or other disaster.

This was expanded further still in England by the 2002 Homelessness (Priority Need for Accommodation) (England) Order to include those:

- aged 16 and 17 years old
- aged under 21 years old who were in local authority care between the ages of 16 and 18
- aged 21 and over who are vulnerable as a result of leaving local authority care
- vulnerable as a result of leaving the armed forces
- vulnerable as a result of leaving prison
- fleeing domestic violence or the threat of domestic violence.

Wales

The 1996 Housing Act refined and expanded the definition of a household in 'priority need' in Wales (and England) so as to include:

- a pregnant woman
- dependent children
- someone vulnerable as a result of old age, mental illness or handicap or physical disability or other special reason
- someone homeless or threatened with homelessness as a result of an emergency such as flood, fire or other disaster.

This was expanded further still in Wales by the 2001 Homeless Persons (Priority Need) (Wales) Order to include those:

- aged 16–17 years old
- aged 18–21 years old leaving care or at risk of financial or sexual exploitation
- who became homeless after leaving the armed forces
- who are former prisoners who became homeless after being released from custody
- fleeing domestic violence or the threat of domestic violence.

Scotland

On 31 December 2012, priority need was abolished by the Scottish Government and all councils across Scotland now have to provide 'settled accommodation' to anyone who is unintentionally homeless.

Single homeless people

If you are a single homeless person (i.e. with no dependent children) it is unlikely that you will be judged to be in 'priority need', unless you are deemed particularly vulnerable. Local authorities should still provide you with advice and information on homelessness and homelessness prevention.

Research for Crisis however, found that in practice this too often doesn't happen. Single homeless people who may be entitled to accommodation are not always given the opportunity to make a homelessness application, many are not provided with any meaningful advice and assistance at all and many are misinformed about their entitlements.[1]

- The above information is reprinted with kind permission from Crisis. Please visit www.crisis.org.uk for further information.

1 Reeve, K. (2011) The hidden truth about homelessness: experiences of single homelessness in England

What causes homelessness?

This content applies to England only.

Every day, Shelter helps people who didn't think homelessness would happen to them. But all it takes is losing your job or falling ill to set things off. That can result in debts racking up, eviction notices or repossession orders, and eventually the loss of a safe and decent place to call home.

The reasons for falling into homelessness vary for each person. But at the root of it are high housing costs, and a housing safety net that doesn't provide the support it should anymore.

We're campaigning to fix this. We want to build a stronger safety net. We want to make sure people can get the stability and security from their home. And that enough decent, affordable houses are being built in the first place. Join us today:

www.england.shelter.org.uk/campaigns/save_the_housing_safety_net

Structural causes of homelessness

Structural causes of homelessness are social and economic in nature, and are often outside the control of the individual or family concerned.

These may include:

- unemployment
- poverty
- a lack of affordable housing
- housing policies
- the structure and administration of housing benefit and universal credit.

These problems require long-term policy solutions. We have to make sure a safety net remains that can help people bounce back on their feet when they fall on tough times. We need to build more genuinely affordable homes to reduce the cost of housing in the first place. And we need to find ways to make private renting more stable and secure.

Help us in our fight to make sure everyone can find and keep a safe place to call home. Join us today.

Personal factors leading to homelessness

A number of different things can lead to an individual or family becoming homeless. These may include:

- family background, including family breakdown and disputes, sexual and physical abuse, having parents with drug or alcohol problems, and previous experience of family homelessness
- individual factors, including personal debts – especially mortgage or rent arrears, poor physical and mental health, relationship breakdown, drug or alcohol problems, or a lack of social support.

Tackling these problems isn't easy, and requires support from public bodies, friends and family, combined with a lot of hard work from the individual or family in trouble. This may include intervention, advice, counselling, training or accommodation provided by the local council.

The most crucial solution is the option of a decent and secure home on a long-term basis, alongside a strong safety net that ensures people can get back on their feet.

- The above information is reprinted with kind permission from Shelter. Please visit www.england.shelter.org.uk for further information.

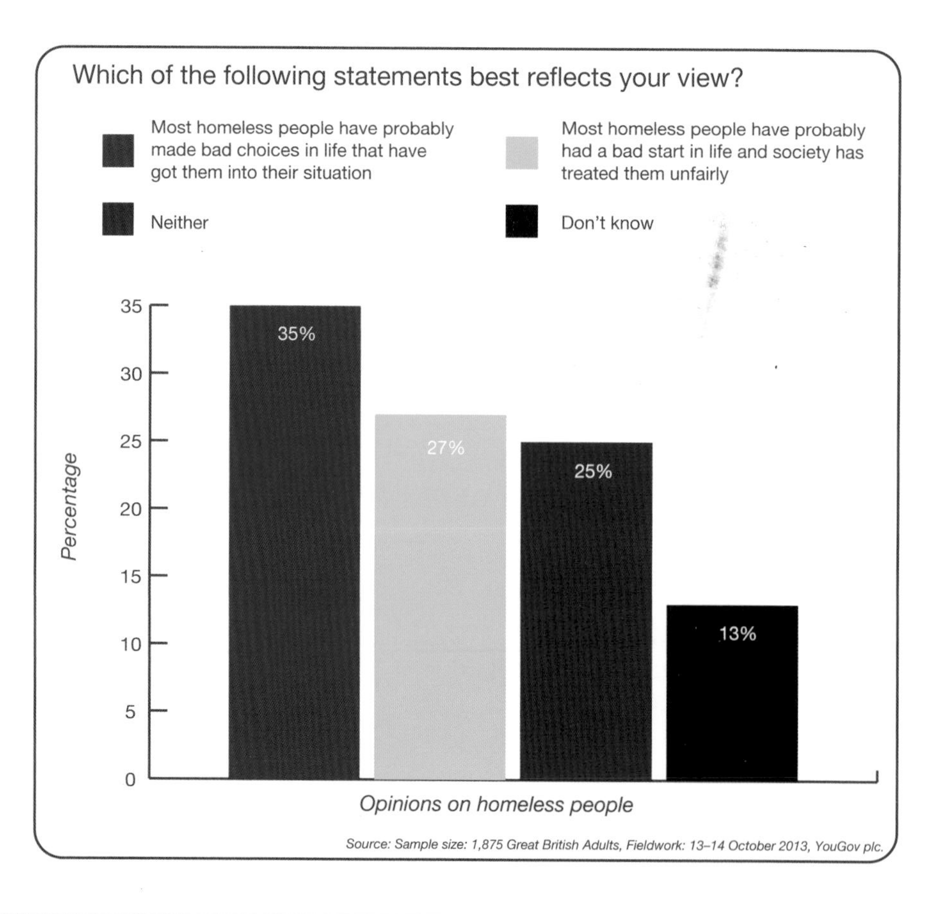

Who is homeless?

Homelessness can affect anyone. In fact when we surveyed the public in 2013, we found that 20% of respondents knew someone who has been homeless and 14% had been homeless themselves.

There is no single reason why someone can become homeless. Its root causes may lie in life events such as bereavement, traumatic experiences during childhood or health problems. It can be triggered by relationship breakdown or losing a job.

Wider factors also play their part. A shortage of affordable homes, poverty, unemployment and rising housing costs can all prevent someone from finding the safety net they need to keep a roof over their head.

When someone actually becomes homeless, it is often a combination of **personal** issues, wider **structural** issues and more immediate **triggers** that have led to them losing everything.

Personal

Some groups of people are more vulnerable to homelessness because they have particular support needs or have fewer rights. You are more likely to become homeless if you have:

- ⇨ been in care as a child or had a disturbed childhood
- ⇨ a mental illness or addiction
- ⇨ been in the armed forces
- ⇨ spent time in prison
- ⇨ migrated to this country from Eastern or Central Europe or arrived as an asylum seeker.

Structural

The political landscape has changed a great deal over the past few years and this has changed the nature of the support available. The cost of living – particularly accommodation costs – has risen and the welfare benefits system is going through the most radical changes since the 1940s. These structural factors all contribute to the risk of homelessness for many people:

- ⇨ shortage of affordable accommodation
- ⇨ reform of the welfare benefits system
- ⇨ unemployment
- ⇨ low income
- ⇨ debt
- ⇨ reduced funding in residential care and community care
- ⇨ migration.

Triggers

It is often a specific life event, or series of events, that will tip a person into homelessness. Common triggers include:

- ⇨ relationship breakdown
- ⇨ domestic violence
- ⇨ leaving home or care
- ⇨ leaving institutions (prison, hospital or the armed forces)
- ⇨ death of a partner
- ⇨ getting into debt, specifically mortgage or rent arrears.

Multiple complex issues

Many people who experience homelessness are struggling to overcome several issues. For instance, in addition to their homelessness, they may have an addiction, poor mental and physical health, and other problems.

For this group, moving on from homelessness can be particularly difficult – partly because each issue will feed into and exacerbate other issues, but partly because the different support agencies involved often do not work together.

According to the Making Every Adult Matter coalition, there are around 60,000 people in this position in England today.

Compared with the general population

A comparison of the experiences of people who are homeless with those in the general population highlights how issues that can lead to homelessness in the first place can also act as barriers to people rebuilding their lives.

- ⇨ **6%** of homeless people are in employment, compared with **70%** in the general population.
- ⇨ **72%** of homeless people experience mental health issues, compared with **30%** in the general population.
- ⇨ **56%** of homeless people have long-term physical health issues, compared with **29%** in the general population.
- ⇨ **26%** of homeless people have drug or alcohol misuse issues, compared with **8%** in the general population.

One size doesn't fit all

Just as there is no single profile that fits every person experiencing homelessness, there is no single solution that will help them turn their lives around.

For some people, homelessness is a temporary problem. They might need no more than a short period in temporary accommodation and the right support to get back into work and a permanent home.

For other people, their immigration status means they are legally entitled to very little or no support, but agencies still have to find a way to work with them.

And there are others for whom homelessness has been an issue for a long time, with periods spent sleeping rough and moving between homelessness services. The approach needed to support these people, particularly those with multiple problems, can be far more specialised, requiring innovative help from a range of services working in partnership.

⇨ The above information is reprinted with kind permission from Homeless Link. Please visit www.homeless.org.uk for further information.

What is it like to be homeless?

This content applies to England only.

Having a home is about more than just the roof over your head. Thousands are living in temporary accommodation, such as hostels and B&Bs, unable to secure a safe and stable home of their own. Others will spend months on the sofas of friends, moving from place to place, never able to settle down anywhere permanent.

At Shelter we help homeless families and households every day, providing advice and support to make sure they can escape homelessness.

If you're in need of help you can get free, confidential advice from Shelter's website.

The experience of staying in temporary accommodation

Unfortunately 'temporary' doesn't always mean what it should. Homeless households may be forced to spend months living in B&Bs and hostels. Some may be forced to move regularly, denied a stable, secure home. Others will be left in overcrowded conditions with their family, unable to get the type of home they need. In addition, temporary accommodation is often more expensive than normal private rented accommodation.

Under current laws, local councils must ensure that suitable temporary accommodation is available for homeless households who are eligible for assistance, in priority need and unintentionally homeless, until settled (i.e. long-term) accommodation can be found.

Such temporary accommodation can include:

- short-term housing leased from private landlords
- hostels run by councils or housing associations
- bed and breakfast hotels (B&Bs)
- housing owned by local councils
- private rented sector stock.

Sleeping on the streets

Sleeping on the streets is traumatic – both mentally and physically. It is dangerous, frightening, and for many it will go on indefinitely. For those forced into this situation it can have long-term negative impacts that will stay with them for the rest of their lives.

Fear of attack

As well as poor conditions and a lack of safety, many rough sleepers have to deal with the fear of being attacked, abused or robbed. In a study carried out by Shelter, rough sleepers reported feeling threatened, not only by others who are living on the street, but also by the general public too.

Effects on physical and mental health

Many factors damage the health of people sleeping rough:

- Cold, hunger and fear experienced by people sleeping rough disrupts their sleep, which in turn damages both mental and physical health.
- Health is damaged through a lack of basic facilities for personal care such as bathing and washing clothes.
- Homeless people often have problems with drugs or alcohol, made worse through being on the street.

The impact of homelessness on children

Homelessness leaves parents at breaking point and children's lives in chaos. The effect of homelessness on children can be long-lasting:

- One study found that four in ten homeless children were still suffering mental and developmental problems one year after being re-housed. [1]
- Poor housing conditions increase the risk of severe ill-health or disability by up to 25 per cent during childhood and early adulthood. [2]
- Children in bad housing are almost twice as likely to suffer from poor health as other children. [3]
- Children living in bad housing are nearly twice as likely as other children to leave school without any GCSEs. [3]
- Mental health problems such as anxiety and depression are three times as common among homeless children who have lived in temporary accommodation for more than a year. [4]

With all these obstacles pitted against them during the years in which they are meant to be enjoying their childhood, children growing up in bad housing often spend the rest of their lives struggling to catch up.

References

[1] Harker, L, Chance of a Lifetime: the impact of bad housing on children's lives, Shelter, London, 2006.

[2] Ibid.

[3] Rice B, Against the Odds, Shelter, 2006.

[4] British Medical Association, Housing and Health, Building for the Future, 2003.

- The above information is reprinted with kind permission from Shelter. Please visit www.england.shelter.org.uk for further information.

Types of homelessness accommodation

There are many types of hostel and supported housing. Different projects accept people with different support needs and they deal differently with applications to stay in them.

Some accept self-referrals (direct applications from the person who wants to stay), some take referrals from any agency and some only take referrals from specific agencies such as the local Housing Options department or outreach teams working with people sleeping rough.

Emergency accommodation

For people who urgently need accommodation:

⇨ Direct access – Short-stay hostels for people who need emergency accommodation, often for people sleeping rough. May take self-referrals or referrals only from specialist agencies working with rough sleepers and homeless people.

⇨ Nightstop – For young homeless people usually aged 16–25. Very short stay (three to five nights). A bedroom in the home of a volunteer host. May accept self-referrals but often only take referrals from specific agencies.

⇨ Domestic violence – Emergency refuges for women escaping domestic violence. Usually accept self-referrals.

⇨ Winter shelter – Basic emergency accommodation available in winter. Often in church halls.

Second stage accommodation

Other accommodation for people experiencing homelessness – often those moving on from emergency accommodation:

⇨ Foyer – For young people (usually aged 16–25) who need support around employment, education and training.

⇨ Housing scheme – For people with fairly good independent living skills. Accommodation in shared houses or self-contained flats with regular visits from support workers.

⇨ Low support – Hostels for people who only need a low level of support with daily living skills. Staff may be on site or may visit regularly.

⇨ Medium support – For homeless people who need a medium level of support with daily living skills. Staff are usually based on site.

⇨ Supportive – For homeless people who need a high level of support and are unable to live independently.

Specialist accommodation

For people with specific support needs as well as housing needs:

⇨ Alcohol and drugs – For people with alcohol or drug problems. Most projects are 'dry' where alcohol is banned, but some 'wet' alcohol projects allow drinking.

⇨ Ex-offenders – For people with a history of offending or at risk of offending.

⇨ Leaving care – For young people leaving local council care.

⇨ Mental health – For people who have mental health problems.

⇨ Single parents – For single parents with a young child or for women who are pregnant. Usually for teenage/young parents.

Innovative accommodation solutions

As the homelessness sector evolves and we improve our understanding of which support works best for people, a number of innovative approaches to accommodation have been developed:

⇨ Housing First – as the name suggests, this approach from the United States is based on securing a long-term home for a person before supporting them with their other issues, such as addictions and poor health. In the Housing First model, people receive continual, personalised support to deal with their issues and sustain their tenancy. This is the opposite of the common approach of guiding a person through various stages of temporary accommodation before judging them ready to move on. There are several Housing First pilot schemes running in England and Scotland.

⇨ Psychologically Informed Environments – a place or service in which the approach of staff is designed to take into account the psychological and emotional needs of the people they work with. The approach can be particularly effective in working with people experiencing the after effects of complex trauma.

⇨ Transforming Choice – this Liverpool based service has developed a new approach from its unique work with the city's most hardened street drinkers, all of whom have passed through other services without success. During a 12-week residency, people are supported through detox, therapy, helped to rebuild lost support networks with family and prepared for independent living. They do not leave until long-term accommodation has been secured for them, which they are subsequently support to sustain.

⇨ The above information is reprinted with kind permission from Homeless Link. Please visit www.homeless.org.uk for further information.

History of homelessness

Early history

For as long as historical records have been kept, Britain has had a homelessness problem. As far back as the 7th century, the English king Hlothaere passed laws to punish vagrants.

William the Conqueror forbade anyone to leave the land where they worked. Edward the First ordered weekly searches to round up vagrants.

The numbers of vagrants has risen and fallen, and precise figures are hard to come by, but we know that 16th-century estimates put the number of vagrants at 20,000 or more. And it was in the 16th century that the state first tried to house vagrants rather than punish them. It began introducing bridewells – places meant to take vagrants in and train them for a profession, but which in reality were dirty and brutal places. By the 18th century, workhouses had replaced the bridewells, but these were intended to discourage over-reliance on state help. At best they were spartan places with meagre food and sparse furnishings – at worst they were unsanitary and uncaring.

The 20th century

The successor to the workhouse was the spike (dormitory housing provided by local boroughs), which was familiar to George Orwell, who stayed in them while researching poverty in Britain.

Some of the more punitive aspects of the workhouses were missing from spikes, but the standard of housing was basic. In the 1930s there were 17,000 people in spikes in the country, and 80 were found sleeping rough during a street count in London.

It was in the 1960s that the nature of homelessness changed and public concern grew. From a post-war low of six people found sleeping rough in London in 1949, the numbers began growing. *Cathy Come Home*, a gritty TV drama about homelessness, helped raised awareness of the problem. Organisations like Shelter and St Mungo's started up. St Mungo's began housing some of the hundreds sleeping rough in the capital.

The roots of contemporary homelessness

By the 1980s around 20,000 people were living in accommodation for homeless single people in London (now provided by charities and housing associations rather than the state). Yet numbers sleeping on the streets had risen to more than 1,000.

Reasons for this increase included new legislation stopping 16- and 17-year-olds from claiming housing benefits. With no way of paying the rent if they ran away from home, they went on the street. In addition, many of the old, crowded impersonal dormitories for homeless people were closed and replaced with hostels with single rooms. While this meant that housing standards rose, the number of available beds fell. And a general increase in the number of people with drink, drug and mental health problems exacerbated the problem. Vagrancy – or to give it its modern term, rough sleeping – was on the increase again.

The Government took action: though it no longer ran hostels, it set up programmes like the Rough Sleepers Initiative and the Homeless Mentally Ill Initiative to fund extra hostels and other services. The number on the street in London fell from over 1,000 to around 600. In 1998, the Government set up the Rough Sleepers Unit to co-ordinate its approach with the efforts of the homelessness charities, and the numbers on the street continued to fall.

The current picture

Supporting People funding

In April 2003, the Government introduced the Supporting People

funding stream, which pays for accommodation-based and floating support services for homeless people and other vulnerable groups – enabling them to enjoy a better quality of life, to live more independently and to maintain their tenancies.

Supporting People is a central government fund paid to local authorities, who then contract services to meet local need.

The new Coalition Government has now de-ringfenced Supporting People funding so that local authorities can spend SP money more broadly. Read more in SP Services *4 facts 4 questions* briefing (January 2011).

Local authority responsibilities

The present system for protecting people from homelessness builds on legislation first passed by Parliament in 1977, and now enshrined in the 1996 Housing Act and the 2002 Homelessness Act. This legislation places certain duties on local authorities to provide settled accommodation to households in priority need, who are not intentionally homeless. The priority needs categories include families with children, some categories of young people, and other people who are considered to be vulnerable due to, for example, a mental health condition.

In March 2005, ODPM published *Sustainable Communities: settled homes; changing lives* – a strategy for tackling homelessness. This strategy acknowledged the significant achievements made in meeting challenging targets to reduce rough sleeping and to end the long-term use of bed and breakfast hotels for families with children. It also set out policies and priorities for preventing homelessness over the next five years.

Our strategic alliance partners Crisis have researched the service people are receiving from councils (May 2011).

Providing accommodation

The £90 million Hostels Capital Improvement Programme (HCIP) was launched in January 2005, with the specific aim of increasing the number of people who move on positively from a hostel or homeless service – for example, to a job or training and a settled home.

The HCIP fund also provided much-needed capital to transform the physical environment of existing hostels, and enabled hostels to remodel their approach to tackling homelessness by providing a pathway off the streets and into independent living. In 2007, Housing Minister Yvette Cooper launched the £70 million Places of Change Programme (PCP) which looked to build upon the success of the HCIP.

Rough sleeping

In April 2008, ten years on from the publication of the Social Exclusion Unit report into rough sleeping, the Government set out a renewed commitment to the original goal to drive rough sleeping down as close to zero as possible. St Mungo's – now St Mungo's Broadway – remains committed to this goal and welcomes the recognition that a new strategy to tackle rough sleeping is needed.

In June 2010, the Coalition Government announced the formation of a new Ministerial working group on preventing and tackling homelessness. A new way of measuring rough sleeper numbers was also introduced in January 2011.

Much good work has been done in London and beyond.

St Mungo's Broadway is involved in the capital with the No Second Night Out initiative as part of the London Delivery Board and is hosting the hub for this at one of our projects.

But homeless and vulnerable people must not be the casualties of cuts to Supporting People (SP) funding, and tough cuts to services could halt homeless people's recovery and lead to more rough sleepers on the streets.

⇨ The above information is reprinted with kind permission from St Mungo's Broadway. Please visit www.mungosbroadway.org.uk for further information.

One in three touched by homelessness

By Max Salsbury

One in three Brits have experienced homelessness or know someone who has, new research has revealed.

And with the number of homeless households having risen by 33% since 2010, the findings by umbrella body Homeless Link also show that eight out of ten believe councils should be doing more to help people.

But with homelessness soaring, the amount of support services available is shrinking.

Since 2010, 133 homeless projects have closed, over 4,000 bed spaces have been lost, the number of full-time staff in the sector has fallen by 16%, while nearly half (47%) of homeless services last year reported an average fall in investment of 17%.

The charity's intelligence suggests investment in services could fall even further. Councils in the last six months have commonly reported cuts of between 25–40% to housing-related support budgets.

According to Homeless Link's data, of those experiencing homelessness, 72% have mental health issues, 56% long-term physical health needs and only 6% are in employment.

With 76% of people agreeing that tackling homelessness is beneficial to their community, the charity has now launched 'Pay it Forward', a campaign calling on councillors to back continued investment in homeless prevention and support in 2014.

Rick Henderson, Homeless Link CEO, said: 'These figures highlight how common the experience of being without a home really is and the impact homelessness has on individuals and communities. Homelessness services play a vital role in helping people rebuild their lives, but can only do so if they continue to receive sustainable long-term funding.

'Whilst we understand the pressure councils are under, we also know that investment in tackling homelessness is in everyone's interest and is backed by the public. Homeless Link is calling for all councils to commit to supporting the innovative projects throughout the country that change lives and benefit society every day.'

Martin Houghton-Brown, chief executive of youth homelessness charity Depaul UK, said: 'We welcome Homeless Link's call for local authorities to continue investing in and funding homelessness services.

'At Depaul UK we are working with young people who, in the majority of cases, have become homeless because of family breakdown, so prevention work is critical. Creating opportunities to resolve relationship difficulties whilst keeping young people safe is not only incredibly obvious, it also works.

'Family mediation prevents homelessness, reconnects young people to their families and is fundamentally an economically sound solution. For the sake of vulnerable young people I am delighted that increasing numbers of local authorities are asking us to build mediation in as an intrinsic part of our pathways of services for young people. We encourage all local authorities to recognise and invest in this, and other, crucial homelessness services.'

17 October 2013

⇨ The above information is reprinted with kind permission from 24dash. Please visit www.24dash.com for further information.

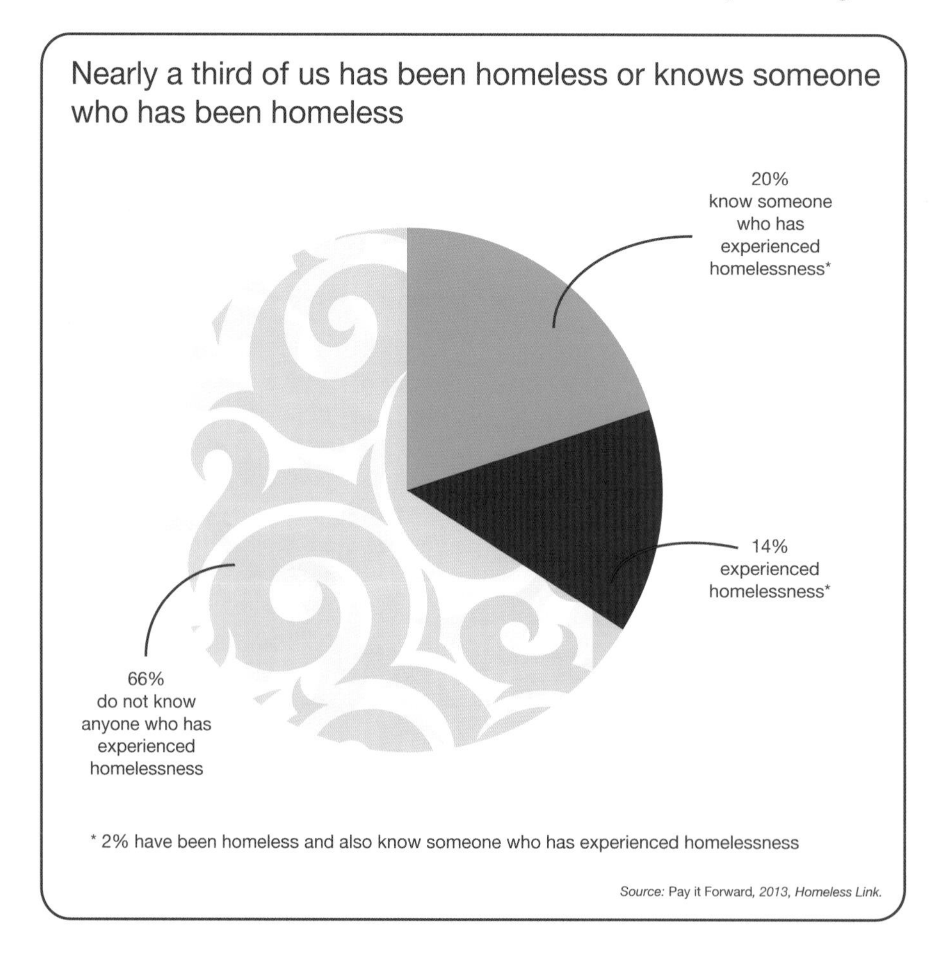

Number of families living in B&Bs on the rise

Benefit cuts and rising household debts have been blamed for an increase in the number of families forced to live in emergency bed and breakfast accommodation.

By Joe Lepper

Latest Government figures show there were 2,090 homeless families with children in bed and breakfast accommodation at the end of June, an increase of eight per cent on the same period the previous year.

Homelessness charity Shelter says major factors in the rise are restrictions on the level of housing benefit families can claim and a lack of support for homeowners facing repossession.

A survey of 4,000 people carried out by the charity in March found that six out of ten working families with a mortgage or in rented accommodation were struggling to keep up with their monthly payments.

Campbell Robb, chief executive of Shelter, said: 'These figures are a wake-up call. Ordinary families are falling through the net and risk losing everything. We're worried about the thousands more just behind them who are living on a knife-edge, where all it takes is a sudden job loss or illness to tip a family into a downward spiral that can put their home at risk.'

Of the 2,090 families living in bed and breakfast accommodation, about a third (760) had been there for more than the statutory limit of six weeks. This is an increase of ten per cent on the same period last year.

Shelter says life for families in such accommodation can involve living in a single room, with no cooking facilities and a shared bathroom.

Robb added: 'We are asking the Government to urgently build up the support available to families who face losing their homes and to protect the safety net that gives families who fall on hard times the advice and support they need to rebuild their lives.'

Housing minister Mark Prisk said the Government had made available £470 million to councils to support those with housing problems.

He added: 'Local authorities are also being supported through the Gold Standard for Homelessness services to deliver high-quality housing solutions for vulnerable people.'

The Gold Standard for Homelessness services is backed by £1.7 million worth of Government funding to councils for housing support services and to train staff.

6 September 2013

⇨ The above information is reprinted with kind permission from *Children & Young People Now*. Please visit www.cypnow.co.uk for further information.

Becoming invisible

By Adam Yosef

The thought of being invisible when you're young seems like a dream come true. To travel the world unseen, walk into sweetshops and enjoy all the candy you can eat, to bunk off school and get up to untold mischief, such is the appeal of owning the power of invisibility.

Of course, as you get older, you accept that the chances of invisibility ever becoming a reality are at best slim, a simple but delightful fantasy with no grounding in reality, at least not in the literal sense. The closest thing in life to becoming invisible in any other sense, you find, is to simply be ignored.

We're all ignored at some point in life. Sometimes deliberately, but usually unintentionally and commonly followed by a near-instant apology. We're all guilty of ignoring someone too. We may ignore because of a short-term dispute, we may ignore due to absent-mindedness but we rarely ignore people simply because they exist... do we?

There are thousands of people out there in the world who are doing this all the time. The majority don't even realise they are ignoring another person, the reason for which is simple: they no longer recognise the ones they're ignoring as 'people'.

When I was younger, the sight of homeless people very much intrigued me. Encountering individuals sleeping rough in shop doorways after closing time, on park benches covered in newspaper or on pavements reaching out to passers-by for some 'spare change' would no doubt stir curiosity in any untapped innocent mind.

But the over-zealous parental need to 'protect' children from what adults have declared 'social ills' conditions them to steer clear of homeless people as if being shielded from a large puddle in the road, an abusive bystander or even a stray dog in the street.

As children grow to become adults, these ideas often remain. They also continue to evolve on a subconscious level. Responding negatively to a request for assistance soon develops into the casual ability to completely ignore a person altogether. The more widely accepted it becomes as a social norm, the less hesitant people become to walk on by without even turning to look at, let alone smile or speak to, the person on the street.

The homeless become street furniture, existing as an unfortunate by-product of a consumer society. Their pleas are drowned in a sea of street calls from newspaper vendors to charity collectors. They become just another voice vying for the attention of people's time and purse; they become another voice to ignore by force of habit. The homeless are no longer the same as 'ordinary' people; they become less than human. They become invisible.

7 March 2012

⇨ The above information is reprinted with kind permission from thePavement. Please visit www.thepavement.org.uk for further information.

Squatting Law, a year on: 69 charged and one jailed for 90 days

Almost 70 suspected squatters have ended up before the courts in the year since it became a crime, HuffPost UK can reveal.

By Tom Moseley

Ahead of the first anniversary of the Government's historic move to criminalise the practice in residential buildings, campaigners said it had been 'utterly absurd' and 'unfair'.

On 1 September 2012, the Government said its new law would 'end the misery of squatting'.

Many of those found guilty were handed fines, typically of around £100, others were given conditional discharges, while some received jail terms of up to 90 days.

Before Section 144 of the Legal Aid, Sentencing and Punishment of Offenders Act 2012, squatting was a civil offence, and homeowners had to go to court to prove people were trespassing on their property.

There were reports of homeowners left powerless after they were locked out of their houses, with so-called 'squatters' rights' proving difficult to overturn in the courts.

Critics said the measure would hit desperate people unable to afford spiralling rent payments.

But the Coalition promised it would 'slam shut the door on squatters once and for all'.

A year ago, the then Tory Housing Minister, Grant Shapps, said: 'For too long, hardworking people have faced long legal battles to get their homes back from squatters, and repair bills reaching into the thousands when they finally leave.

'No longer will there be so-called squatters' rights. Instead, from next week, we're tipping the scales of justice back in favour of the homeowner and making the law crystal clear: entering a property with the intention of squatting will be a criminal offence.'

The data, obtained under the Freedom of Information Act, was provided by the Crown Prosecution Service and covered those charged under it up to July 2013.

Separate figures, obtained from police forces around the country, revealed that 90 arrests had been made outside London since the Act came into force, on 1 September 2012, but fewer than half of those had resulted in charges.

Many forces, including Cheshire, Hertfordshire and Hampshire, had not made a single arrest in the first year, while Kent police, with 27 arrests, had been the most active outside the capital.

London's Metropolitan Police said it did not know how many suspected squatters had been arrested, but said 92 people had been charged or accepted a caution in the first six months of the Act.

A volunteer from the Advisory Service for Squatters, who gave his name as Myk, said the law was 'unfair, and utterly absurd'.

On its website, the group called for protests to mark the first anniversary of the legislation being passed.

'It's gone pretty badly,' Myk said.

'We are hearing from a lot less people. They probably think there is not much we can do for them.

'It's made life a lot more difficult, it's meant that people have been evicted, people have been imprisoned, and people are having to go for less-appropriate places because they are non-residential.

'There are still thousands of empty residential properties that are not going to be put to use.

'They were trying to make life more difficult for people who could not pay London rents.

'The law is unfair, and utterly absurd.'

31 August 2013

⇨ The above information is reprinted with kind permission from *Huffington Post UK*. Please visit www.huffingtonpost.co.uk for further information.

Squatting and the law

Squatting is when someone knowingly enters a residential building as a trespasser and lives there, or intends to live there.

Squatting in residential buildings (like a house or flat) is illegal. It can lead to six months in prison, a £5,000 fine, or both.

A tenant who enters a property with the permission of the landlord, but who falls behind with rent payments, is not a squatter.

Although squatting a non-residential building or land isn't in itself a crime, trespassers on non-residential property may be committing other crimes.

It's normally a crime for a person to enter private property without permission and refuse to leave when the owner asks.

In certain circumstances, it may also be a crime if someone doesn't leave land when they've been directed to do so by the police or council, or if they don't comply with a repossession order.

Source: GOV.UK, 8 November 2013

Rebuilding Shattered Lives: the final report

Getting the right help at the right time to women who are homeless or at risk

Executive summary

'I became homeless because I got pregnant at 14, Mum threw me out and after that I got married. My husband raped me and beat me up. So I ran to London to escape him and have been on the streets ever since.' St Mungo's client

Rebuilding Shattered Lives

Women who are homeless are among the most marginalised people in society.

Sadly, women's homelessness often occurs after prolonged experiences of trauma, including physical, sexual and emotional abuse, frequently within the home. It often follows from and results in a cycle of mental ill health and substance use, and a myriad of other problems. Many homeless women are left grieving for lost childhoods and lost children, and the impact is felt across generations.

These women's histories are full of missed opportunities to get the right help at the right time.

Working with a growing number of women, St Mungo's has realised just how much women's needs differ from those of men. We have also seen how women tend to do less well in support services which predominantly work with and are designed for men. With *Rebuilding Shattered Lives* we set out to change this.

'There is much good practice out there which warrants sharing more widely but we also need new approaches which fit the realities of women's lives today. Our showcase is intended to be a crucible for new ideas which energise policy and good practice.' Charles Fraser, Chief Executive, St Mungo's

Rebuilding Shattered Lives brought together different sectors all working with women who are homeless to share understanding of the particular experiences and challenges women face. We explored how organisations in different sectors are working with women to overcome these challenges, and how we can ensure women do get the right help, at the right time.

Drawing on the expertise of a panel of advisors we invited individuals, services and organisations to submit their experiences, ideas and research across nine themes.

Many thanks to everyone who contributed to *Rebuilding Shattered Lives*, especially to the women who shared their personal stories. We are also very grateful to the support of our expert group who have helped shape our ten key recommendations.

Women's homelessness: why should we be concerned?

Homelessness is a growing problem in the UK. Government figures show that the number of people accepted as homeless grew 10% between 2011 and 2012,[1] and the number of people recorded sleeping rough has risen by 37% since 2010.[2]

Women make up 26% of people who accessed homelessness services in 2013, using approximately 10,000 bed spaces across the UK.[3] 786 women were recorded sleeping rough in London in 2012/13, 12% of the total number.[4] We believe many more women are 'hidden homeless', living outside mainstream support.[5]

With cuts to public services, restrictions on welfare, rising housing costs and a lack of housing supply, there are real fears that homelessness will rise further.[6] Women are likely to be particularly affected by the impact of welfare changes as they are more likely to be dependent on benefit income, including housing benefit.[7] The concern is that we now face a 'timebomb' of women's homelessness.

As homelessness, rises, funding for support services is being cut. Overall, homelessness services reported a 17% reduction in funding in 2013, with the proportion targeted at women falling from 12% to only 8% in the last two years.[8] This is very concerning considering women make up a quarter of people using homelessness services.

The costs of women's homelessness can be devastating for women and their families. These high costs are also felt by the wide range of support services which women come into contact with during their experiences of homelessness.

1 DCLG Live Tables on Homelessness Table 770: decisions taken by local authorities under the 1996 Housing Act applications from eligible households http://www.gov.uk/government/statistical-data-sets/live-tables-on-homelessness

2 DCLG (2014) Rough sleeping in England: autumn 2013 http://www.gov.uk/government/publications/rough-sleeping-in-england-autumn-2013

3 Homeless Link (2013) Survey of needs and provision 2013 http://www.homeless.org.uk/sites/default/files/SNAP%202012%20Final%20180413_2.pdf There are an estimated 39,638 bed spaces for homeless people in the UK. Around 26% of those using bed spaces are women. 26% of 39,638 bed spaces equates to 10,306

4 CHAIN (2013) Street to Home annual report 2013 http://www.broadwaylondon.org/CHAIN/Reports/S2h2013/Street-to-Home-report-2012_20132.pdf

5 Reeve, K; Casey, R and Goudie, R (2006) Homeless women: still being failed yet striving to survive Crisis http://www.crisis.org.uk/data/files/publications/Crisis_Homeless_Women_2006_full_report.pdf

6 Crisis (2013) Homeless Monitor England 2013 http://www.crisis.org.uk/data/files/publications/omelessnessMonitorEngland2013.pdf

7 Fawcett Society (2012) The impact of austerity on women http://www.fawcettsociety.org.uk/we-content/uploads/2013/02/The-Impact-of-Austerity-on-Women-19th-March-2012.pdf

8 Homeless Link (2013) *Survey of needs and provision 2013* http://homeless.org.uk/sites/default/files/SNAP%20213%20Final%20180413_2.pdf

Key findings

Complex and interrelated needs[9]

'We know from our own clients that women who come to our emergency shelters, hostels or into our supported housing have a complex mix of problems. We need to look deeper and try different approaches.' Charles Fraser, Chief Executive, St Mungo's

The overwhelming finding from submissions to *Rebuilding Shattered Lives* was that women who are homeless have a number of severe, interrelated and exceptionally complex problems which contribute to their homelessness and make recovery challenging. The submissions reflected our experience that women tend to enter homelessness and other support services at a later stage than men, when their problems have escalated significantly and they are less ready to begin their recovery journey.

- ⇨ Shockingly almost half of our female clients have experienced domestic violence, and 19% have experienced abuse as a child, compared to 5% and 8% of men.
- ⇨ A third of the women we work with said domestic violence had contributed to their homelessness, compared to 8% of men.
- ⇨ Almost half of our female clients are mothers. 79% of these women have had their children taken into care or adopted. Many are traumatised by the loss of their children and struggle to cope with limited contact.
- ⇨ 70% of women we work with at St Mungo's have mental health needs, compared to 57% of men.
- ⇨ 27% of our female clients have a combination of mental health, physical health and substance use needs (26% of men).
- ⇨ More than a third of our female clients who have slept rough have been involved in prostitution.[10]
- ⇨ Almost half of our female clients have an offending history and a third have been to prison. Over a third of women in prison have nowhere to live on release, women are more likely than men to lose accommodation while in custody.[11]
- ⇨ A survey of homeless women carried out by Crisis found that 37% have no qualifications.[12]

Trying to unpick these needs is challenging, and it's clear that they often can't be addressed separately. Women need support that is easily accessible and responds to the full range of their complex needs; the right help at the right time. This report explores how this can be best provided.

'Women's homelessness is often invisible. I have no contact with my family – I had a very traumatic childhood and don't want to see them. I did a lot of sofa surfing after I left my violent partner. But then I ran out of friends and became homeless.' St Mungo's client

Trauma and abuse

Much of the complexity of women's needs is rooted in histories of violence and abuse often stemming from childhood. It was striking across the different themes just how many women's lives had been marked by physical and sexual violence and how the resulting trauma often erodes resilience to cope with later challenges. Women may turn to drugs or alcohol in order to self-medicate. Involvement in prostitution and offending may follow to fund substance use or indeed survival, resulting in criminalisation and imprisonment. The impact of trauma is undeniably complex and long lasting; it is a recurring theme throughout both this report and the lives of many homeless women.

Relationship with children

Many women who are homeless are separated from their children, and some lose custody of their children permanently. We heard again and again how devastating this separation is for women, yet they are often expected to cope with this loss with little or no emotional support. Services are often ill equipped to understand and respond to the further trauma that arises from separation from children and the internalised shame and guilt of 'failing' as a mother. For many women a failure to address this can be a significant blocking factor in recovery from homelessness and wider issues.[13]

Stigma and shame

Also prominent from the submission was the feelings of stigma and shame experiences by women who are homeless. Women may experience multiple stigmas which experienced concurrently can have a reinforcing, demoralising and debilitating impact. We heard how women feel that society expects them to be feminine, to be good mothers and to maintain a home. Much of what they experience while homeless conflicts with these expectations, and they feel judged as women because they do not meet these ideals. A perceived failure to live up to these expectations can be a significant barrier to recovery.

2014

- ⇨ The above information is reprinted with kind permission from St Mungo's Broadway. All statistics were taken from before St Mungo's April 2014 merge with Broadway. Please visit www.mungosbroadway.org.uk for further information.

9 References to St Mungo's clients taken from the 2013 edition of our Client Needs Survey unless otherwise stated.

10 For the purpose of this report we have used 'women involved in prostitution' as a term that does not define women by the act of selling sex, but also recognises that selling sex is not a job like any other. We are aware that different agencies use different terminology and as part of Rebuilding Shattered Lives we actively sought contributions from a range of different standpoints

11 HM Inspectorate of Prisons and HM Inspectorate of Probation (2001) Through the Prison Gate, London: Home Office

12 Reeve, K; Casey, R and Goudie, R (2006) *Homeless women: still being failed yet striving to survive* Crisis http://crisis.org.uk/data/files/publications/Crisis_Homeless_Women_2006_full_report.pdf

13 Revolving Doors and St Mungo's (2010) Missing families: St Mungo's women and families research: a summary http://www.revolving-doors.org.uk/documents/missing-families/

Public conflicted about homelessness

By Will Dahlgreen

The public tend to think the homeless have made bad choices, and are likely to feel annoyed as well as sorry when asked for money by beggars

It was reported last week that the numbers relying on food banks has tripled in a year, as the Red Cross announced that this winter they will collect and distribute food to the needy for the first time since the Second World War.

New research reveals conflicted feelings about the homeless among British adults.

35% say most homeless people have 'probably made bad choices in life that have got them into their situation', while 27% say they may well 'have had a bad start in life and been unfairly treated by society'. 25% think neither and 13% don't know.

Further controversy over the needy arose this week when an MP reportedly told a one-legged man who asked him for money to 'get a job'.

Many Brits (45%) feel annoyed when someone they don't know tries to ask them for money, while many also feel intimidated (34%), sorry (21%) or guilty (15%).

Older people seem to be firmer in this respect: 49% of over-40s feel annoyed compared to 39% of 18–39-year-olds, and only 11% of over-40s feel guilty compared to 32% of 18–39-year-olds.

A separate survey for *Prospect Magazine* finds that attitudes to the generally poverty-stricken are softer, however. The majority (53%) think that only two in ten or fewer living in poverty have themselves to blame, while 35% say the number is more.

The report into the rise of food banks by the Trussell Trust says rising energy prices and cuts to benefits are likely to force more people to choose between 'heating and eating' this winter. The Government has taken issue with the report, though, claiming that 'three new food banks are opening every week, so it's not surprising more people are using them.'

22 October 2013

⇨ The above information is reprinted with kind permission from YouGov. Please visit www.yougov.co.uk for further information.

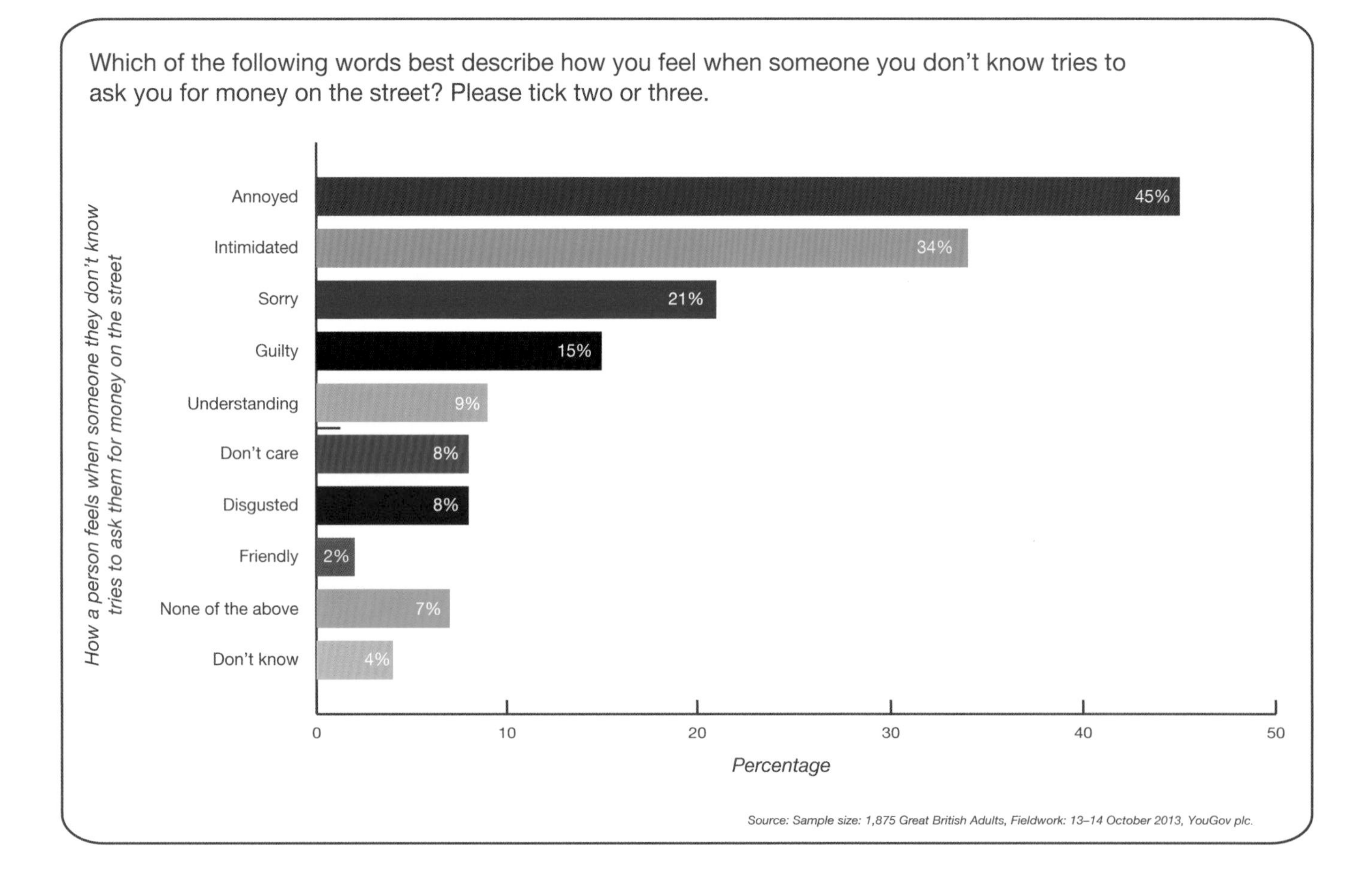

The Big Issue

The Big Issue is a magazine sold by homeless and long-term unemployed people. Vendors buy copies for £1.25 and sell for £2.50. They are working, not begging.

Since *The Big Issue* was launched in 1991 we have helped thousands of vulnerable people take control of their lives. We currently work with around 2,000 individuals across the UK offering them the opportunity to earn a legitimate income; to 'help them to help themselves'.

Over the past two decades the magazine has become synonymous with challenging, independent journalism, and renowned for securing exclusive interviews with the most elusive of superstars. It currently circulates around 100,000 copies every week.

Vendors undergo an induction process and sign up to a code of conduct. They are allocated a pitch and issued with a number of free copies of the magazine. Last year alone we put more than £5 million in the pockets of our vendors, releasing them from a dependence on hand-outs and providing an alternative to begging.

And we don't stop there. Earning an income is the first step on the journey away from poverty and The Big Issue Foundation, a registered charity, exists to link vendors with vital support and services.

Created as a business solution to a social problem, *The Big Issue* has inspired other street papers in more than 120 countries, leading a global self-help revolution.

⇨ The above information is reprinted with kind permission from The Big Issue. Please visit www.bigissue.com for further information.

A *Big Issue*? Your views on homelessness in the UK

Published in eight countries, The Big Issue is the world's highest circulation street newspaper. Founded in 1991, it is produced by professional journalists and given to homeless people to sell on the street as a way for them to earn a legitimate income, and thus help them to reintegrate into mainstream society.

'I feel wary of people selling Big Issue *magazines'*

Those who were of this view said they felt angry that many people selling *The Big Issue* are 'foreigners' who do not speak English.

They also said they held suspicions that sellers were not using the proceeds they make from selling the magazine to improve their situation.

'They are usually younger and more able than me to earn a living. Usually, with a roll-up hanging from their lip and a group of friends waiting for them to score.' Lafrowda, St Just

'I know that *The Big Issue* used to be a force for good, helping many people who found themselves homeless, often through no fault of their own. But I feel that *The Big Issue* has now been hijacked by beggars from other countries, who are taking advantage of our generosity. Because of this, although I used to buy one, I always refuse nowadays.' Jane, Cumbria

'I think many of the sellers should have graduated to real jobs by now if the experience of selling the magazine was encouraging them to learn how to organise themselves for working life. I know at least two sellers who have been selling the magazine from the same street position for many years, at least eight years in one case.' Anon

'I used to always buy one but I stopped when the man I bought from left his normal post; he had found work. I then realised that all the ones who approached me didn't speak English. It has also increased in price so much that I don't think it is good enough value.' Joyce, London

'I'm happy to be approached to buy The Big Issue*'*

Some of you said you were happy to buy *The Big Issue*, mainly because you feel like it's helping the seller, while others said they never bought one but didn't mind being asked.

'I have no negative feelings when being asked to buy *The Big Issue*. I feel largely positive and would consider buying a copy. I feel that it is a worthwhile charity.' Anon

'Generally I have sympathy for their situation, something I do not have for beggars. Most sellers I encounter are polite and do not push for a sale. I have no interest in buying the mag in any event.' Anon

'Because I know they are usually more polite than standard beggars, I am not afraid to say "No, thank you". Sometimes they are so gracious after receiving a no, that it makes me decide to head back to them on my way home and get a copy.' Anon

'I don't mind and sometimes give them the money but don't take the mag.' Biddy, Cheshire

19 June 2012

⇨ The above information is reprinted with kind permission from YouGov. Please visit www.yougov.co.uk for further information.

Homelessness could be a crime under Anti-Social Behaviour, Crime and Policing Bill warns think tank

Homelessness could be turned into a crime under proposed anti-social behaviour laws a think tank has warned.

The Anti-Social Behaviour, Crime and Policing Bill, which featured in the Queen's Speech earlier this month, includes powers to ban certain activities from designated areas.

The Manifesto Club claims these Public Space Protection Orders (PSPOs) are more wide-ranging than the powers they will replace while including fewer checks on their use leaving them open to exploitation.

Josie Appleton, Manifesto Club director, said: 'There is widespread evidence of the over-use of existing powers, which are already too broad and have been employed unjustly to interfere with law-abiding individuals.

'The danger posed by these new powers is substantially greater.

'We believe that the Government has underestimated the potential for abuse of these powers and failed to introduce sufficient checks and balances.'

As currently drafted, the PSPOs could be used by councils for actions including banning spitting, banning homeless or young people from parks, banning begging or rough sleeping and banning smoking in outdoor public places, the group warned.

It also claimed that PSPOs have fewer legal or democratic checks and require less public consultation than alcohol-control zones or dog-control zones.

The orders can also be directed at particular groups, the think tank says, raising the possibility of discrimination.

Appleton added: 'No doubt some local authorities would use these new powers proportionately, but we can be sure that others would not.

'Public Space Protection Orders urgently need to be subjected to additional checks and limitations to ensure that they are used proportionately and do not interfere with the rights of those who use public spaces.'

20 May 2013

⇨ The above information is reprinted with kind permission from *Huffington Post UK* and the Press Association. Please visit www.huffingtonpost.co.uk for further information.

Homelessness and mental health

Good quality, affordable, safe housing is essential to our well-being. Mental health and housing are closely interlinked. Mental ill health can lead to homelessness. Homelessness, poor quality housing and housing insecurity can lead to mental health issues. Mental ill health can also make it difficult for people to maintain good quality housing.[1]

Homelessness and mental health

Mental ill health is common among people who experience homelessness and rough sleepers; estimates range from one third up to 76%. An estimated 43% of clients in an average homelessness project in England are likely to have mental health needs, and 59% may have multiple needs.[1]

The highest rates of mental health conditions are found among rough sleepers and young people who are homeless. They are also least likely to be accessing mainstream health and mental health services and to experience significant barriers in doing so.[1]

Over two thirds of rough sleepers (69%) have both mental health and substance use problems.[1]

Much higher rates of personality disorders (65%), anxiety disorders (40%), anxiety and depression (25%) and post-traumatic stress disorder (25%) are found among people who experience homelessness.[1]

Estimated prevalence of psychotic disorders such as schizophrenia and bipolar disorder among people who experience homelessness range from 2.8% to 42.3%; much higher than in the general population (1%).[2,3]

A high proportion of people in custody have mental health conditions; 72% of male and 70% of female prisoners have two or more mental health conditions and two thirds have a personality disorder. More than a third of St Mungo's clients in London have been in prison, and 43% of ex-prisoners are homeless on release.[1]

People who experience homelessness often fail to receive care and treatment for their mental health conditions for a number of reasons:[1]

- poor collaboration and gaps in provision between housing and health services;
- their mental health needs, while multiple and complex in combination, may not meet threshold for a formal diagnosis;
- failure to recognise that behavioural and conduct problems such as self-harm, self-neglect, substance misuse and anti-social behaviour are manifestations of mental health conditions that require psychological interventions; and
- failure to join up health, social care and housing support services, and disagreements between agencies over financial and clinical responsibility.

References

1. St Mungo's (2009). Down and Out? The final report of St Mungo's Call 4 Evidence: mental health and street homelessness. London.

2. HM Government (2010). State of the nation report: poverty, worklessness and welfare dependency in the UK. London: Cabinet Office.

3. Fazel S, Khosla V, Doll H, Geddes J (2008). The prevalence of mental disorders among the homeless in Western countries: systematic review and meta-regression analysis. *PLOS Medicine* 5 (12) e225.

- The above information is reprinted with kind permission from The National Mental Health Development Unit (NMHDU). Please visit www.nmhdu.org.uk for further information.

Study shows homeless people in England die 30 years younger than national average

Homeless people in England die 30 years younger than the national average according to the most comprehensive study ever on mortality and cause of death in people living rough, in hostels and night shelters, by the University of Sheffield.

Following the research, Crisis – the national charity for single homeless people who commissioned the study – have called for NHS restructuring to consider the needs of people living on the streets.

The report, titled *Homelessness Kills: a study of the mortality of homeless people in England in the 21st century* was carried out by Dr Bethan Thomas of the University of Sheffield's Department of Geography.

Drawing on different datasets, Dr Thomas analysed more than 1,700 deaths in England for the period 2001–2009 to estimate the average age of death not just for rough sleepers, as previous studies have, but for the wider homeless population, including those who reside in night shelters and homeless hostels.

It revealed the average age of death in the homeless population is just 47, compared to 77 years old in the general population. At the ages of 16–24, homeless people are at least twice as likely to die as their housed contemporaries; 25–34-year-olds are four or five times more likely and at ages 35–44, homeless people are five to six times more likely to die.

The research highlights drug and alcohol abuse are particularly common causes of death amongst the homeless population, accounting for more than a third of all deaths.

Homelessness Kills is the first attempt to analyse homeless mortality at the national level for all causes of death and how these differ from the general adult population. It reveals that homelessness is incredibly difficult both physically and mentally and has significant impacts on people's health and well-being. It leads to premature mortality and increased mortality rates. Ultimately, homelessness kills.

Despite these health issues, too often homeless people are being failed by the health system.

The report stresses that the upcoming restructure and reform of the NHS as well as the new duty to reduce health inequalities provide an opportunity to tackle these failings and create a health service that truly works for homeless people.

In light of the findings, Crisis has launched a new campaign, *Homelessness Kills*, calling for:

- The delivery of mainstream health services to be reformed to better meet the needs of homeless people, for example ensuring that vulnerable homeless people are easily able to register with GPs and that no-one is discharged from hospital without accommodation and support.
- Specialist services to be protected and new services to be commissioned by the National Commissioning Board and local Clinical Commissioning Groups, for example services to find and treat tuberculosis and help those with a dual diagnosis of both alcohol and mental health needs.
- The health needs of homeless people to be made a priority in the restructure of the NHS and in particular for the Care Quality Commission to review healthcare for homeless people and recommend improvements.

A snapshot of causes of death amongst homeless people reveals they are:

- Seven times more likely to die from alcohol-related diseases
- 20 times more likely to die from drugs misuse
- More than three times more likely to commit suicide than the general population
- Almost seven times more likely to die from HIV or hepatitis
- Three times more likely to die from chronic lower respiratory diseases than the general population, with an average age of death from this of 56 compared to 76
- Twice as likely to die from heart attacks and chronic heart disease and at an average age of 59 – 16 years lower than the general population which is 75 years old.

Leslie Morphy, Crisis chief executive, said: 'Homeless people are amongst the most vulnerable in our society and it is clear that despite significant investment in the NHS they are not getting the help they need to address their health issues. The Government and health services must do more to improve the health of single homeless people and ensure they can access mainstream and specialist services. If they don't then we fear homeless people will continue to die much younger than the general population.'

Additional information

Crisis

Crisis is the national charity for single homeless people. We are dedicated to ending homelessness by delivering life-changing services and campaigning for change. Our innovative education, employment, housing and well-being services address individual needs and help people to transform their lives. We are determined campaigners, working to prevent people from becoming homeless and advocating solutions informed by research and our direct experience. We have ambitious plans for the future and are committed to help more people in more places across the UK. We know we won't end homelessness overnight or on our own. But we take a lead, collaborate with others and, together, make change happen.

2 October 2012

⇨ The above information is reprinted with kind permission from The University of Sheffield. Please visit www.sheffield.ac.uk/news for further information.

Bin death study launched

The Chartered Institute of Waste Management (CIMW) will call on bin collection companies across the UK to help it tackle the problem of homeless people dying in bins where they have taken shelter while rough sleeping.

Launching a new partnership with waste and recycling company Biffa and StreetLink, a helpline for the public to report rough sleepers to local services, the CIWM said it would be gathering data to provide a more accurate assessment of the problem.

It is understood that all bin collection companies will be asked to fill in a questionnaire, which will ask them to detail so-called 'near misses' and give details of experiences of finding rough sleepers in the bins they have collected. It is anticipated that an awareness campaign for rough sleepers will be developed, based on the research.

CIWM president John Skidmore said: 'There is clearly an issue with rough sleepers in the UK, and we are particularly concerned by those that end up sleeping in waste bins. 'We're seeking to support the sector in research that will assess and understand the problem so we can target interventions that will be able to make a real difference. Last month The Pavement, which has campaigned on the issue for many years, reported on the result of the fatal inquest of one man who died in a bin found in a recycling plant in Tipton, while in Dublin, another man was killed while sleeping in an industrial bin.

A further two deaths are known of in the UK as well as two in Ireland. Biffa said it was committed to raising awareness on the issue, and will continue to train staff to look for people sheltering in bins, as well as putting warning stickers on them urging people to keep out.

9 October 2013

⇨ The above information is reprinted with kind permission from thePavement. Please visit www.thepavement.org.uk for further information.

Youth homelessness on the rise in England

Relationship breakdowns are causing a rise in homelessness among young people, a new Homeless Link study has revealed.

The findings reveal the extent to which rising homelessness is affecting young people aged 16–24.

According to *Young & Homeless* report, a survey of 79 homeless charities and 108 local authority housing services found that, over the past year:

- Nearly half of homelessness services (44%) and councils (48%) have seen an increase in young people seeking help because they are homeless or are at risk of becoming homeless;
- The number one cause for homelessness among this age group is relationship breakdowns with family and friends, and cases of this have increased;
- The majority (62%) of young homeless clients seen by charities were not in education, employment or training, and 46% were in financial difficulties; and
- A quarter of young clients (26%) seen by services had experience of sleeping rough.

The study also looked at how services are responding to increased demand among this age group and their responses highlighted some deep concerns for the sector, including:

- 48% of homeless agencies reported turning away young single homeless people because their resources were fully stretched;
- Nearly one in five local authorities (17%) feel they are not meeting their legal requirements for homeless young people aged 16–17;
- Half of local authorities report using B&Bs as emergency accommodation for young people, despite Government guidelines which advise against their use;
- More than 70% of local authorities said they had no shared accommodation private sector provision for young people, despite this being the only option for young people on housing benefit; and
- 53% of homeless agencies have experienced closures or threats of closure to youth services in their area.

Commenting on the findings, Jacqui McCluskey, Director of Policy and Communications for Homeless Link, the umbrella body for homelessness charities, said:

'With more Government homeless figures due out this week, these findings underline the grim impact that the recession is having on our young.

'With rising youth unemployment, a changing welfare system and many families struggling to get by, youth homelessness is likely to get worse. We can't prevent the recession but we can limit the impact it is having on the next generation.

'The longer someone doesn't have a home, the more likely they are to develop complex problems and become trapped into a cycle of homelessness. If we don't provide access to the right advice, help and support for young people now, we are potentially looking at a much bigger, and more expensive, problem in the future.'

The report makes a number of recommendations to help prevent youth homelessness and reduce the impact that it has. These include:

- Ensuring that changes planned by Government to the welfare system do not cause higher youth homelessness;
- Protecting cost effective advice and prevention services, such as family mediation, from local authority cuts;
- Protect the Supporting People funding which pays for housing related support;
- Finding alternatives to B&Bs to provide accommodation for young people such as Nightstops;
- Making it easier for young people to rent private sector housing and make sure they don't get squeezed out by rising rent costs and increased demand for housing;
- Ensuring that local authority housing and social services' departments work better together to meet their legal requirements to 16- and 17-year-olds; and

- ⇨ Providing better access to education, training and employment for young people who find themselves homeless.

Paul Marriott, Chief Executive of Depaul UK, the UK's largest youth homelessness charity, said:

'For those of us providing services to vulnerable young people facing homelessness, Homeless Link's findings sadly come as no surprise.

'Depaul UK has begun to see a rise in rough sleeping among young people in some parts of the country and we expect this to continue to rise given the continuing squeeze on household income and public expenditure. We are also concerned, given family breakdown is the most significant factor of youth homeless, that more families may buckle under the pressures of the current climate.

'Depaul UK supports all of Homeless Link's recommendations. In particular we would like to see early intervention services not only protected from cuts, but also earmarked for any available funding. Depaul UK's Reconnect family mediation project prevents homelessness in 82% of cases and saves local authorities millions of pounds, yet we struggle to obtain funding for this work. We would also encourage more people to consider providing accommodation for young people in housing crisis through Depaul UK's Nightstop and Supported Lodgings schemes.'

Seyi Obakin, Chief Executive of Centrepoint, said:

'This report shows just how tough the next few years will be for the 1,200 homeless young people Centrepoint supports every year in terms of finding a job and achieving independent living.

'It highlights that more than 60% of homeless young people are not in employment or training and, due to a drop in funding, many young people are being turned away from housing.

'With 400 young people every day across the country knocking on the doors of councils looking for housing and advice, it is clear that the Government must step in and support charities and local authorities to deal with this deepening crisis.'

Lorna Esien, Director of Operations for the homelessness charity St.Basils, said:

'We have seen a definite trend in terms of a significant increase in the numbers of young people presenting as homeless, mainly due to family conflict and overcrowding.

'For the first six months of this 2011, we saw 2,289 young people which is a significant increase on 2010. Over 30% were aged 16/17 and nearly 80 % were Not in Education, Employment or Training.

'As a response to these trends we have in partnership with the local authority and other agencies created a multi-agency Youth Hub, which focuses on preventing homelessness, and intervening early to link young people with a range of appropriate support and accommodation services. As a result we have been able to prevent homelessness in the vast majority of cases.

'We worry that welfare reform could lead to a hardening in the numbers of young people experiencing homelessness. Local authorities must therefore act to protect front line services such as the Youth Hub if this is to be avoided.'

To download the report, visit: www.homeless.org.uk/youth-homelessness.

- ⇨ The above information is reprinted with kind permission from Homeless Link. Please visit www.homeless.org.uk for further information.

Why young people become homeless

Homelessness is not only a housing problem. There are lots of reasons why a young person could become homeless.

Family breakdown

Relationship breakdown, usually between young people and their parents or step-parents, is a major cause of youth homelessness. Around six in ten young people who come to Centrepoint report they had to leave home because of arguments, relationship breakdown or being told to leave.

Many have experienced long-term problems at home, often involving violence, leaving them without the family support networks that most of us take for granted. Read more about the role of family in the lives of homeless young people in our *Family Life* report.

Complex support needs

Young people who come to Centrepoint face a range of different problems. For example, a third of young people at Centrepoint have a mental health problem. Over a quarter of young people at Centrepoint are also known to use or suspected of using illegal drugs, and 13% have a physical health problem.

These problems often overlap, making it more difficult for young people to access help and increasing the chances of them becoming homeless. Read more about the complex needs of homeless young people in our report, *The changing face of youth homelessness*.

Deprivation

Young people's chances of having to leave home are higher in areas of high deprivation and poor employment and education prospects. Many of those who experience long spells of poverty can get into problem debt, which makes it harder for them to access housing.

Gang crime

Homeless young people are often affected by gang-related problems. In some cases, it becomes too dangerous to stay in their local area meaning they can end up homeless. One in six young people at Centrepoint have been involved in or affected by gang crime.

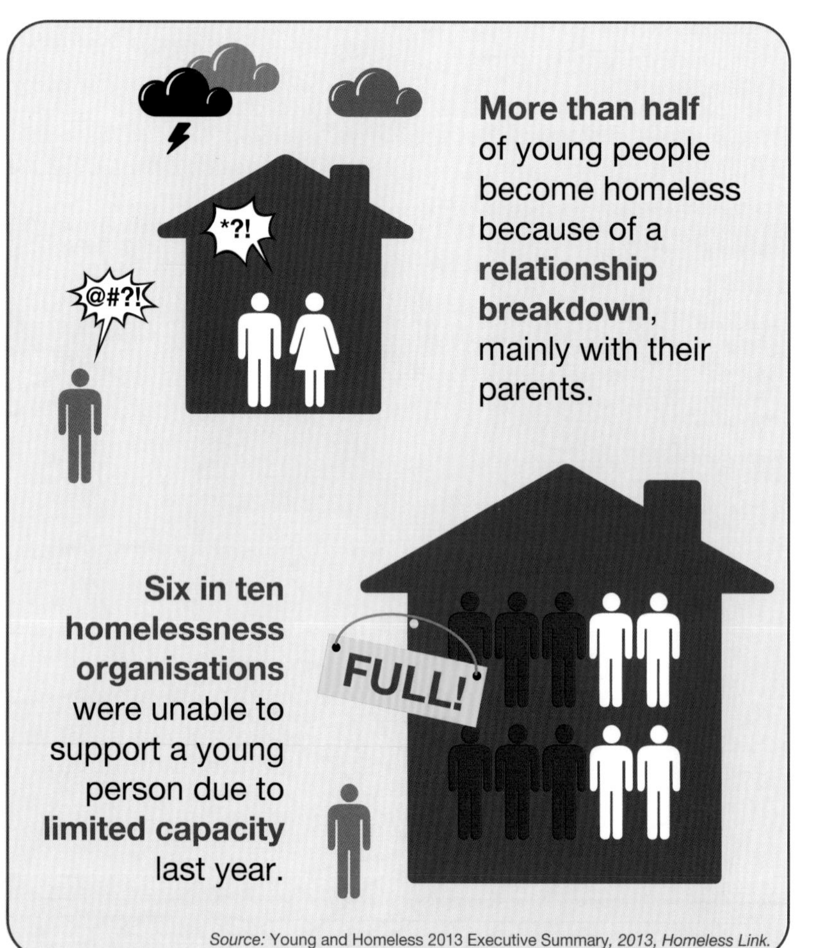

Source: Young and Homeless 2013 Executive Summary, *2013, Homeless Link.*

Exclusion from school

This can make it much more difficult for young people to access help with problems at home or health problems. Missing out on formal education can also make it more difficult for them to move into work.

Refugees

A third of young people at Centrepoint are refugees or have leave to remain, meaning it isn't safe to return home. This includes young people who come to the UK as unaccompanied minors, fleeing violence or persecution in their own country. After being granted asylum, young people can find themselves with nowhere to go and can end up homeless.

⇨ The above information is reprinted with kind permission from Centrepoint. Please visit www.centrepoint.org.uk for further information.

Young and homeless

Over 75,000 young people experience homelessness in the UK each year. One young person shares her story, and explains how the Albert Kennedy Trust put her life back on track.

Young people often get frustrated or impatient about things, from the stress of exams, to what they should wear at a party. However, every year in the UK around 75,000 young people aged 16–24 have more serious concerns to think about: food, shelter and health. Because of circumstances over which they have little say or control, such as family rejection, leaving long-term care, or living illegally in the UK, they have become homeless.

'For over three months throughout the winter I spent my time focusing on finding the basic necessities that most people take for granted, like shelter, food and warmth'

The law requires every council in the UK to house 16- and 17-year-olds who are homeless or are in an unsafe situation. However, once you turn 18, or if you do not qualify for council emergency housing, you could easily fall outside of the law and find that no one has any obligation to provide you with accommodation. This could result in long-term homelessness.

At the age of 16, due to circumstances that weren't my fault, I found myself homeless. Although I was not kicked out of my family home, it had become impossible to continue living there whilst trying to achieve my aspirations and be myself. I had nowhere to go, and as I was deemed to have made myself homeless I did not qualify for emergency housing. For over three months throughout the winter I spent my time focusing on finding the basic necessities that most people take for granted, like shelter, food and warmth.

For shelter I spent my time living in squats in North East London. Squats are unoccupied buildings that groups of people take over and turn into places to live without paying rent. Often squats have no electricity, water or heating.

I also had to find a way of getting food without any income. Skipping, also known as skip diving, is the most common way for homeless people or squatters to feed themselves. Supermarkets are known for throwing out food before its sell by date so going through their bins is a good way to survive in that situation. Most items thrown away are often still in their packaging and edible.

This may sound like an easy, cheap, carefree way to live but after only a few hours of being in the squat I came to realise some of the problems and difficulties. There was a diverse mix of people, from illegal immigrants to hard-core anarchists, long-term squatters to members of the criminal underworld.

Living with people who live such unconventional lifestyles can easily get you involved in situations that can lead to serious trouble. Criminal damage, stealing and drug abuse were an all too common scene in the squats I stayed in.

Living in a squat, with no electricity or heating, many people became dependant on drugs or alcohol for everyday needs. Alcohol is an escape from this way of living and you end up using drugs to keep you awake, to help you fall asleep or to give you a high when you feel low or depressed. These alone can cause psychological, physical and emotional problems. At numerous times I saw people take substance use too far to the point of addiction and unfortunately death.

Eventually I was lucky. I was fortunate to find a charity called the Albert Kennedy Trust, who provide supported lodging for young lesbian, gay, bisexual and transgender young people who have found themselves homeless for a variety of different reasons. The Albert Kennedy Trust place young people with a foster carer whose role is to support them both practically and emotionally, helping them to eventually live independently.

I myself have been placed with foster carers and received help with my emotional and physical health issues from supportive members of the Trust's staff. I am also receiving drugs and alcohol counselling. It's a slow process to recovery but I am now hoping to get back into education to get the qualifications I need to go into university and achieve my aspirations in life.

Looking back, the three months I spent homeless were terrifying and disorientating, educational and life changing. The experience that I gained has been an opportunity to develop myself in many different ways. Facing constant difficulties and challenges has forced me to take full responsibility for my life and make crucial choices that will impact massively on both my present and future. I've learnt from the mistakes I have made, and had to deal with situations I would not wish anyone in the world to have to go through. But this has given me strength to turn my life around.

⇨ The above information is reprinted with kind permission from Headliners. Please visit www.headliners.org for further information.

Making it matter: improving the health of young homeless people

Summary of research into the health needs of young homeless people led by Depaul UK and AstraZeneca under the Young Health Programme.

Executive summary

These are some of the key findings of our research, which was carried out between May and October 2011 and in which more than 380 young people (16–25) participated. A health questionnaire was completed by about 130 young people from Depaul UK services, and by a control group of 200 young people from around the UK. Four focus groups and 26 individual interviews with young people also took place. A group of young homeless people were trained in research skills and carried out research with their peers.

Ethnographic films were made with four young people from Depaul UK services. More than 25 Depaul UK staff members took part in interviews and in regional focus groups. In addition, a steering group of experts guided the research and met to discuss its findings and recommendations.

The context

An estimated 80,000 young people experience homelessness in the UK each year. This fails to account for the growing number of hidden homeless living in poor quality hostels or on a friend's sofa. The main cause of youth homelessness is known to be family breakdown.

Of the young people from Depaul UK services who participated in the research, around half were not in education, employment or training, almost five times as many in the control group. They were at least twice as likely to have moved in the last 12 months.

What are the main barriers to quality care for young homeless people?

Young homeless people do not consider health and health-related issues to be a problem or priority for them: other issues such as the need for housing and employment are more pressing.

Long waiting times lead to a lack of timely care which is especially vital in this group who often seek help, particularly for mental health issues, at the point of crisis.

The transition from paediatric to adult services often leads to a breakdown in continuity of care and challenges accessing adult services.

The web of disadvantage

- 80% of young homeless people are registered with a GP compared to 92% of the control group (a GP appointment costs £36. A Nurse appointment costs £21).
- 48% of young homeless people use cannabis compared to 6% of the control group.
- 40% of young homeless people are likely to be suffering from depression compared to 21% of the control group.
- 27% of young homeless people have a mental health condition compared to 7% of the control group.
- 17% of young homeless people have higher levels of disability compared to 4% of the control group.
- 64% of young homeless people smoke every day compared to 5% of the control group.
- 27% of young homeless people eat less than two meals a day compared to 5% of the control group.
- In the last 12 months, 37% of young homeless people had visited A&E, compared to 14% of the control group (a visit to A&E costs £100.
- 24% of young homeless people had been in an ambulance compared to 3% of the control group (an ambulance call out costs £253).
- 27% of young homeless people had been admitted to hospital compared to 6% of the control group (the average cost of unplanned hospital admittance is £1,400).

Them-and-us mentality – some GPs are perceived to be judgemental and don't always provide the support needed to enable young homeless people to voice their concerns.

Young homeless people often lack confidence, motivation and a sense of purpose which not only negatively affects their mental health but leads to an apathy in seeking care.

Appointments are often short and with different healthcare professionals, meaning issues are not fully addressed and young people often have to recount distressing personal stories repeatedly.

Lack of money to attend appointments is a particular issue due to the transient nature of the lives of the young homeless population.

Chaotic lifestyles can lead to challenges with continuity of care, keeping appointments and implementing healthcare recommendations.

Interrupted and chaotic upbringings have resulted in a lack of knowledge about when and how to seek help.

Some young people have a limited vocabulary to convey health concerns.

Help is often needed out of hours, but not often available.

Key recommendations

For policy makers

We would like national recognition that young homeless people require a more effective, tailored and integrated health service, notably:

- ⇨ Ensuring that organisations such as Healthwatch England and local Healthwatch have the skills and knowledge to engage and consult young homeless people, in order to ensure that they are represented in national and local decisions.
- ⇨ Structured guidance for both voluntary sector organisations and health commissioners to equip them with the knowledge, skills and motivation to engage with one another.

For Health and Wellbeing Boards

We welcome the commitment of the Ministerial Working Group on Homelessness to improving the inclusion of homeless people in Joint Strategic Needs Assessments (JSNAs) by the Health and Wellbeing Boards. To ensure this, we recommend that:

- ⇨ A framework is put in place and monitored to ensure that voluntary and community groups are actively consulted during the JSNA process in order to provide non-clinical data and research. Direct recognition in health and well-being strategies of the complex needs of young homeless people, including strategies to ensure the provision of joined-up services and specialist commissioning for this group.
- ⇨ Cooperation with neighbouring Health and Wellbeing Boards, including pooling budgets where appropriate to ensure the needs of this marginalised population are met.

For commissioners

- ⇨ Integration is key: services for young homeless people should be easily accessible in places such as drop-in centres; specific services for mental health or for substance misuse should not exclude those with multiple needs; and more consideration needs to be given to creating an effective pathway between child and adult services.
- ⇨ Each Clinical Commissioning Group should have an officer accountable for homeless healthcare.

For AstraZeneca and Depaul UK

- ⇨ Increase training and resources for Depaul UK staff in supporting young people with mental health issues, including ongoing support.
- ⇨ Improve the links between Depaul UK services and clinical health services from both sides, through education and local relationships.
- ⇨ Build upon Depaul UK's activity and skills programmes, to ensure that young homeless people have access to appropriate resources that will impact upon physical and mental health and well-being, including the opportunity to participate in a wide range of positive activities, and to access peer-to-peer support.

Depaul UK is committed to ensuring the participation of young people in developing our responses to existing and emerging health needs.

Recommendations from peer research

- ⇨ Integrate services to prevent young people repeating themselves and accessing multiple services
- ⇨ Raise awareness on issues of homelessness in schools and for front line workers such as: Health care and council staff
- ⇨ Ensure sustainable funding for voluntary sector organisations that support young people
- ⇨ Support and provide family mediation services to prevent youth homelessness
- ⇨ Cut down on waiting times for counselling and support.

April 2012

- ⇨ The above information is reprinted with kind permission from Depaul UK. Please visit www.depauluk.org for further information.

Teenage runaways are at risk of sexual exploitation

Barnardo's is calling on the Government to urgently and thoroughly analyse the risks faced by runaway children and the level of support provided, as a new report reveals they are in danger of being sexually exploited.

The research, which also shows that running away can take place when a child has already been sexually exploited, was produced in partnership with Paradigm Research.

With more than 77,000 children running away each year, the report demands that the Government, police and local authorities take seriously the risks faced by runaway children and work together to assess and raise awareness of this issue.

A total of 41 runaways, from a range of backgrounds, were interviewed for the report and their experiences starkly demonstrate the variety of reasons why children choose to run away and how easily they can find themselves at risk.

A total of 19 children were found 'on the streets' in areas where young people tend to congregate such as parks and where food is given to homeless people.

Most of the 41 children were receiving some form of support at the time of the research. However nearly half, 17, were not receiving any help to address their running away or sexual exploitation.

The report makes a wide range of recommendations including how to raise awareness of running away and child sexual exploitation and ensure knowledge is successfully and appropriately shared.

Barnardo's director of children's services, Sam Monaghan, said:

'The stories of these young people paint a bleak picture of the realities facing children who run away. The vulnerability of these children makes them easy prey for criminals who want to manipulate them for their own means.

'When a child runs away it should act as a warning to everyone concerned with their welfare. We need to proactively look for these children and act decisively to stop them falling into situations which can leave their lives spiralling out of control.

'The ease with which the author of the report was able to find young people is a sobering reminder to us all. It is essential we get to these children first, because if we don't then those who want to abuse them will.

'It is paramount that we do not overlook the vulnerability of children who run away from home or care. Regardless of the length of absence it is essential that the vulnerabilities of all children are considered and that we take the time to listen to them and everything they tell us is taken seriously.'

The researcher and author of the report, Emilie Smeaton, said:

'This research fills an important gap in our knowledge and provides an evidence base that demonstrates the links between running away and child sexual exploitation.

'It is essential that we do more to increase awareness of these issues and ensure that measures are effectively set in place nationally and locally to respond effectively to the needs of vulnerable children.'

Lily, one of the young people interviewed for the report, said:

'If kids are on the street, if they run away or their parents kick them out, there are men out there who will take advantage of them and 'cos you've got nowhere else to go, you'll have sex with them. It's better than sleeping out and getting raped by someone you don't know who could do anything to you.'

16 July 2013

⇨ The above information is reprinted with kind permission from Barnado's. Please visit www.barnardos.org.uk for further information.

Charities urge rethink on plan that could drive up youth homelessness

Plans to penalise low income families for having young adult job seekers living at home could drive up homelessness, leading housing and homelessness charities warn today.

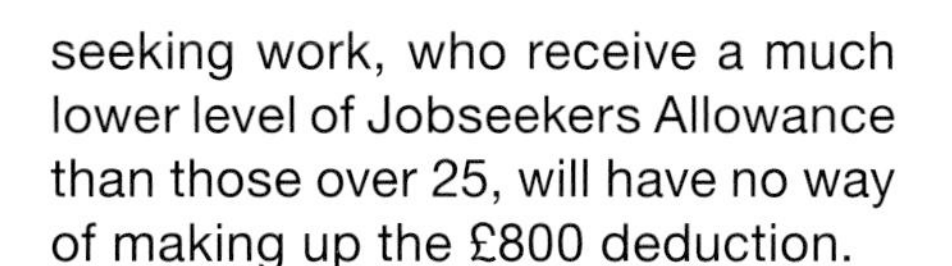

Government proposals being voted on today (Monday) will see £800 a year cut from housing benefit paid to parents or guardians where there is a young person under 25 seeking work. Current rules make a deduction only if the young person is in employment.

The move comes at a time when over 600,000 young people are unemployed and not in education and when rising housing costs are forcing more to remain in the family home. The latest figures from the ONS show one in three men under 34 now lives at home, along with one in six women.

Homelessness charities Crisis and Shelter are warning that this will put additional pressure on low income families already struggling to keep a roof over their head. Young people seeking work, who receive a much lower level of Jobseekers Allowance than those over 25, will have no way of making up the £800 deduction.

The proposal which would come into force later this year under the new Universal Credit is likely to cause tension in the poorest households. It could result in family breakdown and young people being forced out of the home, undermining their chances of finding work and lead to homelessness.

It could also cost the taxpayer more money as under-25s who were living with their parents may have no choice but to make a housing benefit claim of their own.

Significantly, the move would be directly at odds with the Government's 'bedroom tax', which will reduce the housing benefit payments of people in social housing deemed to have spare bedrooms. It means that parents with grown-up children who are looking for work will face a lose-lose situation with their housing benefit reduced whether their children move out, leaving their room 'spare', or stay at home.

The charities are calling on the Government to urgently rethink these proposals so that young people struggling to find work aren't faced with a choice between finding £800 a year or leaving their family home with nowhere else to go.

Leslie Morphy, chief executive of Crisis, said: 'With young people already facing high unemployment, now is not the time to be heaping yet more pressure on them and their families. Young people will be forced from their homes before they're ready and many will end up homeless – costing us more not less.

'Together with the "bedroom tax" this move will mean many parents are penalised whether or not their grown-up children move out of home.'

Campbell Robb, chief executive of Shelter, said: 'It's disgraceful that young people who have to live at home because they cannot afford to live independently should be penalised for it. It will simply leave many young people without a roof over their head.

'In the current economic climate young people need to be supported to get back into work, not forced to bear the brunt of further cuts to the housing safety net. Tragically it seems inevitable that we'll see an increase in youth homelessness as a result.'

11 February 2013

⇨ The above information is reprinted with kind permission from Crisis. Please visit www.crisis.org.uk for further information.

Young people present manifesto at Youth Homeless Parliament

The Foyer Federation had the privilege of accompanying a team of young people from across the network to The Youth Homeless Parliament on 6 December to present The Foyer Federations Manifesto, followed by lively debate.

By Hollie Kane

The Youth Homeless Parliament is a platform for 16- to 25-year-olds who have experienced homelessness to influence national and regional policy and services. The Foyer Federation is one of eight organisations involved including YMCA, Centrepoint, Crisis, Depaul UK, Forum Housing, St Mungo's and St Basils.

The event was hosted by conservative MP Kris Hopkins, Minister for Housing and Local Growth at the Department for Communities, and Liberal Democrat MP Stephen Williams, Minister for Communities at the Department for Communities.

Young people from each organisation had the opportunity to present their Manifesto to the MPs and MPs responded, this was followed by open questioning; there was so much to talk about that Kris Hopkins and Stephen Williams were late for their next appointments!

'Overall the day was fantastic and feel very privileged to have had the opportunity to go to the Houses of Parliament to talk to MPs about homelessness and how it affects young people in so many different ways. The day also was a very big help for me personally because if you were to ask me six months ago to stand in front of 100 other young people and Members of Parliament then I would not have put myself forward for speaking, so now I feel just that bit more confident for the next time I have to speak in front of a large number of people.'

– Seb, spokesperson responsible for presenting the Manifesto

Our Manifesto

1. Government Policy is deficit-based looking to fix the 'problem' that is young homeless people.

⇨ Funding should be channelled to encourage young people to develop talents and skills.

⇨ Restrictions should be lifted from those young people aged over 19 years who are in supported accommodation.

⇨ All young people in supported accommodation should be able to access training courses and claim support with their housing costs.

2. Vulnerable young homeless people are pushed through the supported accommodation system too quickly and go on to fail.

⇨ 18 months should be the minimum timescale for a hostel or foyer placement.

⇨ No further cuts to funding for staff.

⇨ Further consultation with young people about realistic timescales for services.

3. The benefits system is failing those most in need of it. We want to work but need help whilst we learn the skills needed.

⇨ Do not remove Housing Benefit for those under 25.

⇨ Review schemes for helping young people get into work. Make them offers which offer opportunity whilst inspiring and unlocking the talents of the future.

⇨ Invest in young people to develop these essential skills. The savings in the future will outweigh the costs.

15 January 2014

⇨ The above information is reprinted with kind permission from The Foyer Federation. Please visit www.foyer.net for further information.

Tackling homelessness

Housing homeless in shipping containers?

An odd, and pretty grim concept; however, Brighton Housing Trust have seen how this can be a viable solution for homeless people.

By Laura Matthews

Brighton Housing Trust will begin work with QED over the next four weeks to turn shipping containers into accommodation for homeless people. Brighton Housing Trust's chief executive, Andy Winter said that when the idea was first presented to him he thought it was 'either April Fool's Day or we had lost all concept of decency'.

However, this type of work has already been used in The Netherlands by Tempohousing and after viewing these images, Mr Winter soon realised something great could be achieved.

The trust is developing 36 studio flats within two block using adapted shipping containers within the town centre. The units have been designed and constructed in Holland specifically for a social housing project in Amsterdam that failed due to funding difficulty, says Mr Winter in an article for *The Guardian*.

The room sizes would be the same as if they were sharing; however, each person would get their own kitchen, bathroom and front door.

This concept has rarely been used in the UK; however, there are examples of this across Europe. The most notable project is in Amsterdam and the development of 1,000 was created in the same way as the ones in Brighton will be.

The project has a great sustainability perspective as the accommodation units can be transferred to other locations should the need arise.

24 October 2013

⇨ The above information is reprinted with kind permission from Support Solutions. Please visit www.supportsolutions.co.uk for further information.

Homeless fall between healthcare cracks, but fresh approaches can help them

By Geordan Shannon, PhD Candidate in Epidemiolgy and Public Health at University College London

My partner and I volunteered at a homeless shelter last month – the idea being to channel our spare time and seasonal spirit into something community-focused and productive.

I've worked in many inner-city and over-burdened Accident & Emergency departments overseas, so thought I had a good grasp of challenging most stereotypes, including ones about the homeless. But that went flying out of the window once I actually met the guests at the shelter and when I thought about the experience afterwards.

One of these is that although the word 'homeless' conjures up images of people sleeping on the street, there are many people in different situations. These include those who have no permanent home (sleeping on sofas at friends' houses maybe) or who are temporarily accommodated at a long-term shelter.

The UN identifies two categories: primary homelessness, or sleeping rough; and secondary homelessness, those with a roof over their head but no place of usual residence.

Go figure

Between July and September 2013, 28,380 applications for housing were made to local housing authorities in England, of which 13,330 were approved. A sample also revealed that 57,350 households in England were in temporary accommodation as of 30 September 2013. And it's estimated that more than 2,300 people slept rough around England last year, with about a quarter in central London.

Housing applications aside, it's extremely difficult to find accurate statistics on the prevalence of homelessness; people may be difficult to identify given a lack of contact with routine services.

When it comes to rough sleepers, information from the CHAIN database estimates that 6,437 people in London slept rough at some point during the 2012–2013 financial year. The data also tells us the majority were male (88%) and aged between 26–45 years (58%). Just under half were UK nationals (47%) and 11% were aged under 25.

All these figures above give us some idea of the size and diversity of the problem, and perhaps how we might start to provide the right care and health services for homeless people.

A rough life

Rough sleepers are at increased risk of dying – and dying prematurely. Research from Canada that studied those in shelters and those outside them, estimated that mortality rates in rough-sleeping youths were between nine and 31 times higher than in the non-homeless population. Other healthcare challenges (and sometimes the very conditions that precede homelessness) include mental illness, drug and alcohol abuse. It's estimated that around 41% of homeless Londoners have specific support needs relating to alcohol, 28% to drugs, and 44% to mental health. And are 35 times more likely to commit suicide.

Not only are homeless people at risk of premature death, but they also suffer disproportionately from a number of chronic health conditions including tuberculosis, seizures, chronic obstructive pulmonary disease and skin and foot problems.

The severity of diseases are often advanced because of the delay in presenting to a health professional, inability to complete a full course of treatment, or other factors such as poverty, mental impairment and the consequence of living a chaotic life with regular change.

Complex life, complex needs

On the whole, the health needs of the homeless population are extremely complex and not adequately addressed by mainstream healthcare and access to it. Getting to a doctor, for example, might call for transport they don't have, or there may be difficulties in getting prescriptions. And when you're trying to survive or find shelter, these take priority over getting help for an infected wound.

As Jeffrey Turnbull and colleagues put it:

'[homeless people] are discouraged by a system that works for others but that works against them … negotiating a complex healthcare system is almost impossible for many … These problems are not unique to healthcare: they apply equally to the housing, judicial and social systems.

'Help is sporadic. Often, the first point of call is the local emergency department, which is geared for high-turnover and acute care, not towards complex health and social needs. Those who end up there have longer stays, a higher triage category, and are more likely to require ambulance transport. One study suggested that homelessness was the most significant predictor of repeat visits.'

Ways forward

A traditional model of healthcare has not and will never suit most homeless people or rough sleepers. But with more understanding of what these needs actually are, better communication and outreach, and some creativity, it's possible that even an overburdened and time-short health system could do better.

It is interesting to reflect on a randomised trial from 1995 that identified compassionate care as a key way to address homeless people's needs, improve their experience of healthcare, and reduce visits to emergency departments. Shifting focus towards issues of housing and social support has also been found to reduce the burden of regular visits to A&E.

Another innovative approach is Find and Treat, a service for homeless and other marginalised people with tuberculosis in London. Tuberculosis (TB) is a disease of poverty and inequality, and is transmitted especially in conditions of overcrowding and inadequate ventilation. The homeless population is especially susceptible, and often have difficulty seeking hospital-based diagnosis and with compliance to six months of therapy if diagnosed.

The service consists of a mobile, multi-disciplinary team, which finds cases of TB in the community through outreach services. And the unit also provides a digital X-Ray service for rapid diagnosis.

Winter is a rough time of year, especially for homeless people. When most of us are at our lowest point of health over the colder months, it is important to reflect on those who are much more vulnerable. While their health needs are complex, there are opportunities to help more. And in keeping with what the healthcare profession aims to do, we can practise compassion, understanding and humanity towards others.

21 January 2014

⇨ The above information is reprinted with kind permission from The Conversation. Please visit www.theconversation.com for further information.

Salisbury home for veterans up and running

Local charity Alabaré is reporting a very successful start to its latest Home for Veterans in Salisbury. The home, which provides accommodation for up to five Armed Forces veterans at a time, was full within a few weeks of opening.

Alabaré is the UK's largest provider of specialist accommodation for veterans outside of London.

After leaving the army, veterans can find themselves facing all manner of issues. In contrast to the structure of army life, ex-servicemen find themselves having to budget, often for the first time in their lives, and can sometimes fall into debt. Others may struggle with finding new employment. Whilst some find that the scars they've brought home aren't physical, but emotional. Alabaré's Salisbury Home for Veterans looks to support ex-service personnel to overcome these issues and make a successful transition to their civilian lives.

James* arrived at the Alabaré home straight from out of the army, and has now set his sights on higher education. Having recently secured a place at Loughborough University to study a BEng in Electronic and Electrical Engineering, he will be leaving Salisbury to pursue his studies and a new career as soon as term starts.

Graham's* relationship with his partner and children had become strained since returning home, but with the help of the Alabaré scheme, he has been able to access support, and now finds it easier to communicate with his family. He has a much brighter outlook for the future and is actively seeking work.

Simon* found himself unemployed and separated from his partner and children after returning to civvy street. He had lost all motivation in life, a situation exasperated by a complicated wrist injury. With emotional support and help managing his debts, he is now on his way to becoming a taxi driver, and is spending more time with his children.

Quotes

Janet Herring, Alabaré's Care & Support Director:

'It's fantastic to see such positive results at this early stage of the scheme. Credit is due to the hard-working staff and volunteers of our Veterans Home, and the determined residents who are now experiencing deserved success with their goals.'

Alongside their homes in Salisbury, Alabaré run four other Homes for Veterans programmes: in Plymouth, Bristol, Weymouth and Hampshire (Gosport and Fareham), providing high-low level support for homeless or vulnerable ex-Armed Forces personnel. Since the scheme started in 2009, the charity has helped over 210 veterans.

**Names changed.*

20 August 2013

⇨ The above information is reprinted with kind permission from Alabaré Christian Care & Support. Please visit www.alabare.co.uk for further information.

The potential for empowering homeless people through digital technology

Introduction

The digital age has radically transformed how we communicate, work and conduct our friendships and relationships. Mobile and digital technology has become ubiquitous in society and is often held as a contemporary embodiment of – or even prerequisite for – social inclusion and connection. Smart phones, mobile Internet and social networking sites provide a means of instantly reaching out to loved ones, accessing services and information and sharing experiences, thoughts and feelings with the world.

The impact of digital technology upon the social, emotional and practical lives of homeless people and those experiencing exclusion and disadvantage, however, is unknown. Although recent research suggests that many homeless people carry a mobile phone and place great value in having access to the Internet, little was known about how these resources are typically used. Until now, the potential to harness new and emerging digital technology to improve and enrich the lives of excluded people has not been comprehensively explored.

Supported by the Lankelly Chase Foundation, Lemos&Crane are working with homelessness charity Thames Reach to develop insight and guidance on how digital technologies can engage and empower homeless people. The research will explore how digital technology can be used to improve the lives of vulnerable people by giving them a voice, enhancing and expressing their capabilities, facilitating peer-to-peer support and making the services they receive more personalised and enabling. This paper reviews the benefits, problems, and opportunities that digital technology entails for homeless and vulnerable people.

Digital media is becoming an increasingly important part of everyone's lives. It is used for socialising, to find information, to apply for jobs, and to voice and share opinions. The increasing dependence on digital media is believed to be leaving homeless and vulnerable people behind. In some cases, this is true: many homeless people struggle with digital literacy and opportunities to find work, transport and housing are limited when resources are increasingly available only online.

But this (vast oversimplification of the) problem is not unalterable. Many homeless people do own or have access to digital technologies and many of those who do not would consider learning more skills. Charities, councils, community centres, religious organisations and homeless people themselves are working to provide other homeless people with access and the means to use computers, mobile phones and the Internet.

It is vital to understand how these digital technologies are used in order to offer appropriate service, support and resources to homeless people. It has been argued that the social connections that would enable a homeless person to get off the street are gradually replaced with the social connections necessary to survive on the street.[1] Smart phones increasingly merge methods of communication (such as e-mail, calls, texts and social media) with other activities (such as Internet searches, online newspapers, games, radio and music). If there ever was a distinction, is it still possible to distinguish between the different roles of digital technologies in this transformation? How does ownership and usage differ with gender, age and time on the street? How is usage perceived by the public? How can digital technology be used to avoid harassment by the police and the public?

When homeless and vulnerable people have access to digital technologies and develop the skills to use it, many are enthusiastic to learn more, to engage with design projects, to join online debate, and to use these skills to empower themselves and others. Homeless people are increasingly developing and producing their own technologies and engaging with each other on micro-blogging sites such as Twitter. Improved digital literacy lessons and better advertising of available resources will allow those who want to learn to do so.

Where homeless digital exclusion does exist it is rarely the result of choice or of itinerant or chaotic lifestyles, but is a problem of access. Only through sustained efforts to ascertain and respond to homeless people's needs can current services become used and useful. Until then, the effects of digital exclusion – problems with communication, employment and shelter – will define many homeless people's experiences.

Conclusion

The pervasiveness of digital technologies does not necessitate the exclusion and disadvantage of homeless people. In fact, new technologies can allow vulnerable people the means for communication, education and increased independence. Itinerant lifestyles do not automatically result in digital exclusion. On the contrary, digital technology can be used to solve some of the problems a chaotic lifestyle can entail. Many homeless people are digitally hungry and are empowered when given the opportunity to engage with new technologies.

It is charities', councils' and other service providers' responsibilities to ensure that as many homeless people as possible have access to digital technologies. Further to this is training which ensures users are competent, confident and safe in the use of these technologies.

In this way, homeless people will have increased chance of finding housing, employment, food, and relationships that are likely to provide stability, comfort and confidence. Give a man a fish, and you feed him for a day; teach him how to fish, and you feed him for a lifetime. By providing homeless people with the means to access the wealth of opportunities inherent in digital media, service providers can enable homeless people to enhance their own lives and potentially dramatically change their situations for the better.

Reference

1. Le Dantec, C. A., and Edwards, W. K. (2008, April). Designs on dignity: perceptions of technology among the homeless. In *Proceedings of the SIGCHI conference on human factors in computing systems* (pp. 627-636). ACM.

⇨ The above information is reprinted with kind permission from Lemos&Crane. Please visit www.lemosandcrane.co.uk for further information.

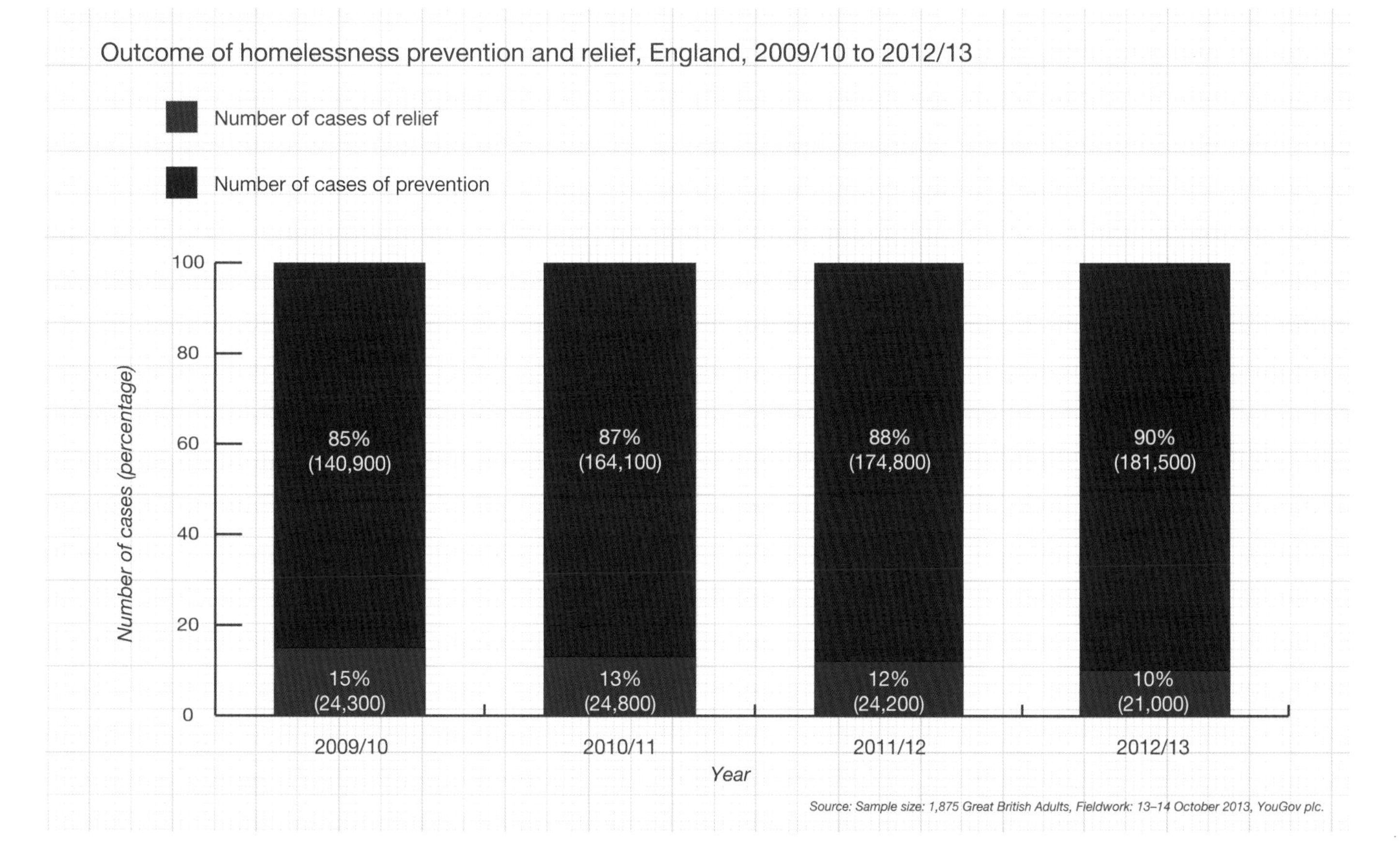

Public use 'good deed app' to help 4,000 rough sleepers off the streets

A year on from the launch of StreetLink, over 4,000 rough sleepers have been offered support and services to help get them off the streets.

Housing Minister Kris Hopkins today (10 December 2013) hailed the StreetLink service, which has directly helped 4,000 rough sleepers in the first year since its launch, a success.

Members of the public have been using the StreetLink app, phone line and website to inform local authorities about vulnerable people in their area. Outreach workers have then been able to get in touch with rough sleepers to offer the support they need to get their lives back on track.

Mr Hopkins said StreetLink showed the power of combining technology with the goodwill of the British public. He urged people to use StreetLink's 'good deed app' over the Christmas period and colder months to help connect more rough sleepers with the right advice and services.

Giving people a way to help

Over the last year there have been almost 11,000 alerts to local services; and half of those who have used StreetLink have never helped a rough sleeper before.

Polling has also shown that the British public have a vast desire to help – but are confused about the best way to do so.

StreetLink, run by charities Homeless Link and Broadway with support from the Government, offers a 'valuable alternative' to a cash handout for people sleeping rough, enabling the public to provide practical help in just a single step.

On a visit to StreetLink today, Mr Hopkins met staff providing the vital link between incoming calls and getting the support to the people who need it. He heard from the team about the way in which the service was helping to turn people's lives around.

Housing Minister Kris Hopkins said:

'I am determined that every effort is made to tackle rough sleeping and get more support to vulnerable people. It is encouraging to see that through StreetLink over 4,000 rough sleepers have been offered support and services to help them get off the streets.

'Part of the reason StreetLink has been so successful is because the app and phone line make it easy to help a person sleeping rough, not with a cash handout but with the valuable alternative of practical support.

'Christmas is the season of goodwill, and as the cold weather kicks in, I urge anyone concerned about a rough sleeper in their area to download the app and get in touch with StreetLink.'

Rick Henderson, Chief Executive of Homeless Link, said:

'The service is enabling so many people to help rough sleepers for the first time. It's very encouraging to see new technology being used as a real force for good in this way.'

If you're concerned about a rough sleeper in your local area, call 0300 500 0914 or visit www.streetlink.org.uk – and help them get the support they need.

Howard Sinclair, Chief Executive of Broadway, said:

'I'm delighted that in its first year, StreetLink has already made such a difference.

'It's great to see the British public coming together to help homeless people in their local communities. But more needs to be done – and quickly. As temperatures drop, it's crucial we all act to help those left out in the cold.'

Those looking to offer help can call 0300 500 0914 or go to www.streetlink.org.uk to put those sleeping rough in touch with services who can help them get support and safe accommodation.

Rough sleeping in London

- In 2012/13, outreach workers saw 6,437 people sleeping rough in London – a 13% increase compared to 2011/12.
- In London in 2012/13, 4,353 people (68% of the total mentioned above) were seen sleeping rough for the first time.
- 10% of those seen sleeping rough had returned to the streets after a period of at least one year when they were not contacted rough sleeping.
- Of those seen sleeping rough, 47% were of UK nationality, 28% were from Central and Eastern Europe and 12% were from other European countries.
- Those who slept rough were mainly male (88%).
- Only one in ten rough sleepers was under the age of 25.
- Outreach teams and No Second Night Out helped 2,794 people seen sleeping rough into accommodation or to return to their home area.

Source: Street to Home Bulletin 2012/13,Combined Homelessness and Information Network (CHAIN).

No Second Night Out

The Government's support for StreetLink is part of efforts to prevent and tackle rough sleeping and get more support to vulnerable people. This includes the £20 million Homelessness Transition Fund that has helped charities reach over 14,000 people across the country by offering help with issues including accommodation, health and jobs.

The funding is also helping to roll out the 'No Second Night Out' pledge across the country. Started in London, this innovative scheme helps rough sleepers off the streets immediately, with the aim that no one should spend more than one night on the streets.

Further information

Launched in December 2012, StreetLink is a website, telephone service and app that enables individuals to alert local authorities in England when they are concerned about someone sleeping rough, and is the first step someone can take to ensure rough sleepers are connected to the local services and support available to them: www.streetlink.org.uk/0300 500 0914. StreetLink is run by the charities Homeless Link and Broadway and funded by the Department for Communities and Local Government and the Greater London Authority.

Public desire: in a Populus poll of 2,099 UK adults, nearly half (48%) of all adults said they feel guilty when they see a rough sleeper and don't know the best way to help and 46% would welcome an easy way to take action. (November 2012).

StreetLink users: in a survey of 546 people who have used the StreetLink service, 47% of respondents said they had never helped a rough sleeper before using StreetLink. Of those who had, most had given food or money, 86% of users would recommend the services (Homeless Link July 2013).

10 December 2013

⇨ The above information is reprinted with kind permission from GOV.UK. Please visit www.gov.uk for further information.

One night's sleep a small sacrifice to make for UK's homeless young people

By Seyu Obakin, CEO of Centrepoint

Every year in the UK, 80,000 young people experience homelessness, a fact known to too few but one that should trouble all of us.

Tonight members of the public in eight cities will make their feelings known by giving up their beds and spending a night on the street in the largest national Sleep Out of its kind.

The 2,000 people expected to bed down at events from Edinburgh to Southampton, Norwich to Cardiff, are doing so to not only make people think again about those they see every day, but also ensure that homeless young people can find the help they need through charities like Centrepoint and our partners across the UK.

Because leaving homelessness behind takes more than just a safe place to stay. The £750,000 participants aim to raise tonight will help give homeless young people a future, whether that's through Llamau in Cardiff, The Rock Trust in Edinburgh, The Society of St James in Southampton, The Amber Foundation in Bath, St Edmund's Society in Norwich or Keyhouse and the Young People's Support Foundation in Manchester.

Young people must make the most of the opportunities, but the money raised will provide the vital support in tackling health problems, accessing training and employment and the life skills a 16–25-year-old, who may never have benefited from a stable family environment, learn the skills to live independently.

Sleep Out doesn't pretend to replicate the experience of rough sleeping or the mental impact of homelessness on a young person. It is impossible for the thousands of people who will take part tonight to come remotely close to experiencing the loneliness and desperation too many still face every night – whether bedding down on the pavement, a night bus, in a disused building, in a B&B or on the latest of a seemingly endless chain of sofas.

But it can spur people to action, whether that is giving their time, their money or their advice as a mentor.

By coming together nationally, once a year, those taking part can throw a spotlight on the barriers facing young people. Yes, they will do so by spending just one night on the streets, but without demanding the attention of the media and the public as a group of charities we will struggle to take the true scale of homelessness in the UK from the concern of a knowledgeable minority to a national debate.

It has never been more important that we do so. High youth unemployment, welfare reforms and reductions in Government grants to local councils have made it increasingly difficult for young people to find work or housing at truly affordable levels. And if homeless young people are to truly turn their lives around they need two things above all else: a home and a job.

Tonight will not end youth homelessness, but it will set us on the road to finally ending a blight which affects 80,000 too many young lives.

Centrepoint Sleep Out is raising funds to give homeless young people a future, safe place to stay and the support they need this winter. Visit http://www.centrepoint.org/xmas to see how you can get involved.

10 December 2013

⇨ The above information is reprinted with kind permission from *Huffington Post UK*. Please visit www.huffingtonpost.co.uk.

Don't give the homeless money, call this hotline, says Minister at charity launch

Giving money or food to a homeless person won't do them any good, the Housing Minister has said, as welfare charities launch a 'homelessness hotline' billed by the Government as an alternative to hand-outs.

By Charlie Cooper

StreetLink is a new national helpline for members of the public concerned about a rough sleeper in their area. Backed by 500 homelessness charities, operators will pass on information about a homeless person's location and circumstances to support services in their area, which will then offer them targeted help.

'People don't sleep on the streets by choice. The more people are aware that there is something out there for them the better'

The scheme, which has been trialled successfully in London, Liverpool and Manchester since last year, is backed by the Housing Minister Mark Prisk, who urged people to offer 'a hand-up, rather than a handout'.

'Most people know that giving money or food won't help a rough sleeper find a home, get the healthcare they need, or simply put them in touch with the support available to make sure they don't become entrenched in the lifestyle of living on the streets,' Mr Prisk said. The Government is providing £250,000 funding for the helpline.

Matt Harrison, from the charity Homeless Link, which is managing the project, said that the question of giving money to homeless people was 'a matter of conscience'.

'There are people who have worked with homeless people for years who still routinely give spare change and there are people equally experienced who prefer not to and will put people in touch with services instead,' he said. 'What we're providing through StreetLink is something to do instead, or as well. Phone up our helpline or go to our website and tell us that there is someone sleeping rough in your area and we'll put them in touch with their local authority and see what can be done to help them.'

The number of people living on the streets has soared since the recession. According to the most recent official figures, nearly 2,200 people were sleeping rough on any one night in Autumn 2011 – up by a fifth in one year. The next set of annual figures, compiled by the Department of Communities and Local Government, will be released in February and some charities fear another sharp increase.

Mr Harrison said that anecdotal evidence from homeless shelters suggested that cuts to benefit payments, along with uncertainty about the scale of future welfare reform, has led to private landlords evicting people on short-hold tenancies.

'That indicates that landlords are concerned about whether people have sufficient benefits to cover their rent,' said Mr Harrison. 'We don't know what the impact of the other welfare reforms will be but we're concerned about it.'

However, Mr Harrison said he was hopeful that helpline pilot schemes carried out in areas with high levels of homelessness had already lowered the homeless population. In London, the 'No Second Night Out' trial has led to 70 per cent of new rough sleepers in 2011 spending only one night on the streets, compared to 54 per cent in 2010.

Case study

Shaun Collins, 53, was sleeping rough in a Barking churchyard for three weeks earlier this year. A paramedic alerted No Second Night Out and he was taken to an Islington hostel. Today he is moving into rented accommodation in East Ham.

'I ended up homeless because of a relationship breakdown. My wife moved out after only a few months and left the country and I'm now in an expensive legal battle with her. I had to move in to a bedsit and then moved from one friend's home to another. I was depressed and drinking too much. I wasn't happy in the home I was living in but had nowhere to go – so I moved out and slept rough. I didn't have a clue what services were out there. I didn't know anywhere I could go. The people from No Second Night Out gave me the time of day. Now I'm registered with six or seven employment agencies. In the New Year I'm hoping to be able get work again on building sites. We all make mistakes and I think everybody deserves a second chance. People don't sleep on the streets by choice. The more people are aware that there is something out there for them the better.'

To let StreetLink know about a homeless person in need of help in your area call 0300 500 0914 or visit www.streetlink.org.uk.

11 December 2012

⇨ The above information is reprinted with kind permission from *The Independent*. Please visit www.independent.co.uk for further information.

Rough sleepers find their dream jobs as top chefs

A London hotel is in line for an award for its scheme to help the homeless train as five-star cooks.

By Tracy McVeigh

Proudly wearing starched and spotless chef's whites, Michael Oliver and Andrzej Smorolzusla look the part in the kitchens of the five-star boutique hotel in the City of London. But, like their colleague Majdop Sadiq, who can point directly out of the elegant windows of the Andaz Liverpool Street to the doorway where he slept rough, they were until very recently living on the streets, hungry and homeless.

'It is strange at first, when you are homeless; all you want is somewhere quiet to lay your head. You come in here and all I could think of is how they could fit a single bed in the toilet,' said Oliver, 35.

These men are part of a remarkable new partnership that may win the Andaz a major award for corporate responsibility this week, and which is at the cutting edge of a small but growing band of businesses that are looking to a more progressive kind of philanthropy.

'We didn't start off intending to staff our kitchens with homeless people,' said the Andaz's director of human resources, Carlos Paniagua. 'We were giving donations of toiletries and towels at first to the homeless charity Providence Row. Then we got chatting to them about what they needed and started sending out our chefs to run workshops in catering and cooking. Our staff were getting a lot out of it, we were bringing in a culture of social responsibility to the hotel that was good for everyone. So the next step, the biggest step, was to bring Providence Row clients here to train.

'But we made sure everyone was happy and on board with it, because of course it is a risk. We didn't want to risk the hotel customers and we didn't want to risk the clients of Providence Row. I said from the first that, if our chefs don't want it, if they are not happy, it stops. We took it very slowly and cautiously. But it is working very well.'

It's working so well that the hotel has been shortlisted for this week's Lord Mayor's Dragon Awards, a scheme set up to tackle the accusation that City of London businesses have thrived while doing little or nothing for the poverty-ridden communities on their doorstep.

Andaz's head chef, Hameed Farook, has been waiting for such an opportunity for years. 'For 15 years I've gone to work, got paid, taken care of my family. Now I have a chance to do something more. I get a lot out of working alongside the homeless and my chefs do too.

'They say it has opened their eyes, made them see how lucky they are, how close the line is.'

Dominic Gates, a manager at Providence Row, says he, too, was wary at first. 'I thought chefs were all Gordon Ramsay and shouting and screaming at people. But they have made our clients so welcome, whether here or in workshops at Providence Row.'

Oliver came to the hotel for a two-month placement, but has proved himself and had it extended. 'My understanding of homelessness is that it means more than someone who has no place to sleep; it is the stories behind that person, the reasons that everyone is in that position. It's not self-pity,' said Oliver.

'I hope a full-time job comes up soon that I can go for. When I came here I thought people would look down on me because of my position, maybe think homeless people are unhygienic, but of course they have standards you must meet and when customers see you in the open-plan kitchen they do not see a homeless person, just a chef.' Not all the Providence Row trainees will get full-time work after their placements, but they do get a boost to their self-esteem and the ongoing full support of the team from Providence Row.

Smorolzusla, 52, a former professional footballer in his native Poland, was on London's streets for two years when building work dried up. He now has a full-time job at the Andaz Liverpool Street.

Sadiq is a refugee from the war in Darfur. He fled Sudan after helicopter gunships attacked his village, burning it to the ground. In the chaos he became separated from his wife and parents, and ended up stowing away on a ship. He had no idea where it was going until it docked at Dover weeks later. Racked with tuberculosis, suffering from post-traumatic stress disorder, penniless and alone, Sadiq, now 47, ended up on the streets. 'I had a room, but the council asked me to vacate it as I was not a priority case,' he said.

Picked up by Providence Row, Sadiq was helped back into housing and began training in catering at the Andaz. He was also helped to contact the Red Cross, which found his wife in a refugee camp. 'We were united and started our lovely life. I love to cook, to be in a kitchen. Who can think this can be ahead when you are homeless?'

29 September 2013

⇨ The above information is reprinted with kind permission from *The Guardian*. Please visit www.guardian.co.uk for further information.

Key facts

- ⇨ There were an estimated 1,247 people sleeping rough in 2009 and 1,768 people sleeping rough in 2011. 51,640 households were in temporary accommodation on 30th June 2012. (page 1)
- ⇨ About one in ten rough sleepers are women and around 45% of households accepted by local authorities as having priority needs for housing, and 41% of households in temporary accommodation, are single women with dependent children. (page 2)
- ⇨ In a typical day around 3,615 women and 3,580 children are supported in a refuge-based service in England. (page 2)
- ⇨ 6% of homeless people are in employment, compared with 70% in the general population. (page 5)
- ⇨ 72% of homeless people experience mental health issues, compared with 30% in the general population. (page 5)
- ⇨ 56% of homeless people have long-term physical health issues, compared with 29% in the general population. (page 5)
- ⇨ 26% of homeless people have drug or alcohol misuse issues, compared with 8% in the general population. (page 5)
- ⇨ One study found that four in ten homeless children were still suffering mental and developmental problems one year after being re-housed. (page 6)
- ⇨ Children living in bad housing are nearly twice as likely as other children to leave school without any GCSEs. (page 6)
- ⇨ One in three Brits have experienced homelessness or know someone who has. (page 10)
- ⇨ Since 2010, 133 homeless projects have closed, over 4,000 bed spaces have been lost, the number of full-time staff in the sector has fallen by 16%, while nearly half (47%) of homeless services last year reported an average fall in investment of 17%. (page 10)
- ⇨ Of the 2,090 families living in bed and breakfast accommodation, about a third (760) had been there for more than the statutory limit of six weeks. This is an increase of ten per cent on the same period last year. (page 11)
- ⇨ A third of the women [St Mungo's] work with said domestic violence had contributed to their homelessness, compared to 8% of men. (page 15)
- ⇨ Almost half of [St Mungo's] female clients are mothers. 79% of these women have had their children taken into care or adopted. Many are traumatised by the loss of their children and struggle to cope with limited contact. (page 15)
- ⇨ More than a third of [St Mungo's] female clients who have slept rough have been involved in prostitution. (page 15)
- ⇨ Almost half of [St Mungo's] female clients have an offending history and a third have been to prison. (page 15)
- ⇨ 35% say most homeless people have 'probably made bad choices in life that have got them into their situation', while 27% say they may well 'have had a bad start in life and been unfairly treated by society'. 25% think neither and 13% don't know. (page 16)
- ⇨ Many Brits (45%) feel annoyed when someone they don't know tries to ask them for money, while many also feel intimidated (34%), sorry (21%) or guilty (15%). (page 16)
- ⇨ The average age of death in the homeless population is just 47, compared to 77 years old in the general population. (page 20)
- ⇨ The majority (62%) of young homeless clients seen by charities were not in education, employment or training, and 46% were in financial difficulties. (page 22)
- ⇨ 48% of homeless agencies reported turning away young single homeless people because their resources were fully stretched. (page 22)
- ⇨ Although recent research suggests that many homeless people carry a mobile phone and place great value in having access to the Internet, little was known about how these resources are typically used. (page 34)
- ⇨ In 2012/13, outreach workers saw 6,437 people sleeping rough in London – a 13% increase compared to 2011/12. (page 36)

Glossary

Begging
A beggar is someone who makes money by asking for donations from passers-by. Although begging and homelessness can be linked, not all rough sleepers beg or vice versa.

The Big Issue
A weekly magazine sold by homeless people in the UK. Launched in 1995, the money made from magazine sales is used to benefit homeless people.

Bin death
Sometimes homeless people turn to sleeping in bins as a way to seek shelter and warmth. Unfortunately, these bins can be picked up by waste lorries, where the contents are loaded onto the on-board crushing equipment which can crush someone to death.

Hidden homelessness
In addition to those people recognised as statutory homeless there are also a large number of homeless single adults, or couples without dependent children, who meet the legal definition of homelessness but not the criteria for priority need. In many cases they will not even apply for official recognition, knowing they do not meet the criteria. Statistics provided by the Government will therefore not include all people in the country who actually meet the definition of homelessness. As a result, this group is often referred to as the hidden homeless.

Homeless households
A family or individual who has applied for local authority housing support and been judged to be homeless.

Homelessness
The law defines somebody as being homeless if they do not have a legal right to occupy any accommodation or if their accommodation is unsuitable to live in. This can cover a wide range of circumstances, including, but not restricted to, the following: having no accommodation at all; having accommodation that is not reasonable to live in, even in the short-term (e.g. because of violence or health reasons); having a legal right to accommodation that for some reason you cannot access (e.g. if you have been illegally evicted); living in accommodation you have no legal right to occupy (e.g. living in a squat or temporarily staying with friends).

Homelessness and mental health
Mental health and housing are closely interlinked: mental ill health can make it difficult for people to maintain good quality housing and can lead to homelessness, whereas homelessness, poor quality housing and housing insecurity can lead to mental health issues. Mental ill health is common among people who experience homelessness and rough sleepers – estimates range from one third up to 76%. An estimated 43% of clients in an average homelessness project in England are likely to have mental health needs.

Hostels and nightshelters
Hostels and nightshelters provide housing for people sleeping on the streets.

No Second Night Out (NSNO)
Launched on 1 April 2011, this is a project in London that aims to ensure that someone sleeping rough for the first time need not spend a second night out on the streets. NSNO helps people to return to their home area and be reconnected with their family and support networks. It is estimated that each week about 60 people are seen sleeping rough for the first time in London.

Priority need
Under homelessness legislation, certain categories of household are considered to have priority need for accommodation. Priority need applies to all households that contain a pregnant woman or are responsible for dependent children; to some households made up of a 16- to 17-year-old or a care leaver aged 18 to 21; or where someone is vulnerable, e.g. because of old age, health problems; or by having been in prison, care or the Forces.

Rough sleeping
A rough sleeper is a homeless person who is literally 'roofless' and lives predominantly on the streets.

Runaway(s)
Generally, but not exclusively, a term used to describe a young person who has run away from home.

Single homeless
This term refers to homeless individuals or couples without dependants.

Sofa surfing
When a person finds themselves without accommodation they rely on family and friends to put them up temporarily, usually sleeping on their sofa or floor, whilst they try to find more permanent accommodation.

Squatting (Squatting law)
If a person is said to be squatting, it means they are occupying a properly without the right to do so (e.g. they don't pay rent or own the property). Trespassing and squatting in residential buildings (like a house or flat) is illegal and is considered a crime (can lead to six months in prison, a £5,000 fine or both).

Statutory homelessness
In England, people who are accepted by local authorities as being officially homeless, and who are deemed to have a priority need, are referred to as statutory homeless. Local authorities have a duty to accommodate people who are statutory homeless, as long as they also have a local connection and have not made themselves homeless intentionally.

Street homelessness
Often confused with rough sleeping, street homelessness is actually a much wider term, also taking into account the street lifestyles of some people who may not actually sleep on the streets.

Assignments

Brainstorming

⇨ In small groups, brainstorm what you know about homelessness. You should consider the following:

- What is the definition of homelessness?
- What is the difference between statutory homelessness and single homelessness?
- What are the common causes of homelessness?
- What are some of the challenges that homeless people face?
- Where can a homeless person find help and support (e.g. which organisations and charities can they turn to)?

Research

⇨ What is the No Second Night Out scheme? Create a short presentation on their work and be sure to include statistics and interesting facts.

⇨ Research homelessness charities in your area. What kind of help and support do they provide?

⇨ Investigate how homelessness is tackled in other countries around the world. What measures do you think are most effective in helping the homeless?

⇨ Plan a fundraiser for a homeless charity. Try to come up with a novel way of raising awareness of this issue that will involve the whole community.

Design

⇨ Draw what you consider to be a stereotypical homeless person and label it. Compare your drawing with a friend's. Reflect on why you drew what you did and ask your friend why they drew what they did. Are your ideas based on fact or assumptions?

⇨ Shipping containers have been turned into accommodation to help the homeless and there is also a backpack that folds out to be a tent. Can you invent something that will help tackle the problem of homelessness?

⇨ Create a leaflet that shows how digital technology can help and empower homeless people. You might find *The potential for empowering homeless people through digital technology* (pages 34 and 35) helpful.

⇨ Design a poster which will let people know where they can turn to if they find themselves without accommodation and homeless. Be sure to include phone numbers and links to websites.

Oral

⇨ 'Giving money or food to a homeless person on the street won't do them any good.' Discuss this statement as a class.

⇨ Create a poster which shows the common causes of homelessness. You might find including some statistics very helpful.

⇨ Choose one of the illustrations from this book and, with a partner, discuss whether you feel it successfully represents the article it accompanies.

⇨ Do you think there is a stigma surrounding homelessness in the UK? Discuss in small groups.

⇨ What could the Government do to help improve employment opportunities for homeless people in the UK? Discuss with a partner. You might get some interesting ideas by reading *Rough sleepers find their dream jobs as top chefs* (page 39).

Reading/writing

⇨ Write a list detailing your daily routine, from the moment you get up to when you go to sleep. How would this routine change if you had no home?

⇨ Read *What is it like to be homeless?* (page 6). Write a blog post from the point of view from a rough sleeper about what it is like to be homeless.

⇨ 'A house is built with walls and beams; a home is built with love and dreams.' This saying is often seen on greetings cards and kitsch household items. What statement is it trying to make? What do you think makes a home? Create a list of the most important qualities of a home.

⇨ Watch the film *The Pursuit of Happyness* (2006) (12a), starring Will Smith. How realistic do you think this portrayal of homelessness is?

⇨ Watch the film *The Soloist* (2009) (12a), starring Jamie Foxx and Robert Downey Jr. Write a report discussing how the film represents the issue of homelessness and mental illness and the link between them.

⇨ Read *A Street Cat Named Bob* by James Bowen. How does this book portray life on the streets and the realities of homelessness?

⇨ Read *Oliver Twist* by Charles Dickens. What can the novel tell you about how attitudes to poverty and child homelessness have changed since Dickens' time?

⇨ Why do you think many homeless people have previously been in an institution: for example, in prison, care or the Armed Forces? Write an essay exploring this question (no more than two sides of A4).

Index

Acknowledgements

The publisher is grateful for permission to reproduce the material in this book. While every care has been taken to trace and acknowledge copyright, the publisher tenders its apology for any accidental infringement or where copyright has proved untraceable. The publisher would be pleased to come to a suitable arrangement in any such case with the rightful owner.

Images

Cover, page iii and page 12 © Andrew Kudrin, pages 8 & 9: iStock, page 11: Karen Bryan, page 19: iStock, page 21 © Dominic Alves, page 28 © Ira Gelb.

Illustrations

Don Hatcher: pages 29 & 34, Simon Kneebone: pages 18 and 31, Angelo Madrid: pages 1 & 23.

Additional acknowledgements

Editorial on behalf of Independence Educational Publishers by Cara Acred.

With thanks to the Independence team: Mary Chapman, Sandra Dennis, Christina Hughes, Jackie Staines and Jan Sunderland.

Cara Acred

Cambridge

May 2014